7 to 12 Months
Making Sounds, Making Music, and Many Other Activities for Infants

Creative Resources Infant and Toddler Series

Dedication

THIS BOOK IS DEDICATED TO:

My grandchildren, Jeffrey and Eva Herr.

J. H.

My son, Randy, and my nieces and nephews.

T. S.

7 to 12 Months
Making Sounds, Making Music, and Many Other Activities for Infants

Creative Resources Infant and Toddler Series

by

Judy Herr Terri Swim

PHYSICAL

COGNITIVE

EMOTIONAL

LANGUAGE & COMMUNICATION

SOCIAL

DELMAR
CENGAGE Learning

Australia • Brazil • Japan • Korea • Mexico • Singapore • Spain • United Kingdom • United States

7 to 12 Months: Making Sounds, Making Music, and Many Other Activities for Infants: Creative Resources Infant and Toddler Series
Judy Herr and Terry Swim

Business Unit Executive Director: Susan
  L. Simpfenderfer

Acquisitions Editor: Erin O'Connor

Editorial Assistant: Ivy Ip

Executive Production Manager: Wendy
  A. Troeger

Production Editor: Joy Kocsis

Technology Project Manager: Joseph Saba

Executive Marketing Manager: Donna J. Lewis

Channel Manager: Nigar Hale

Cover Design: Joseph Villanova

Composition: Stratford Publishing Services, Inc.

For product information and technology assistance, contact us at
Cengage Learning Customer & Sales Support, 1-800-354-9706

For permission to use material from this text or product,
submit all requests online at **cengage.com/permissions**
Further permissions questions can be emailed to
permissionrequest@cengage.com

Library of Congress Control Number: 2002031238

ISBN-13: 978-1-4018-1839-5

ISBN-10: 1-4018-1839-0

Delmar
Executive Woods
5 Maxwell Drive
Clifton Park, NY 12065
USA

Cengage Learning is a leading provider of customized learning solutions with office locations around the globe, including Singapore, the United Kingdom, Australia, Mexico, Brazil, and Japan. Locate your local office at:
international.cengage.com/region

Cengage Learning products are represented in Canada by Nelson Education, Ltd.

For your lifelong learning solutions, visit **delmar.cengage.com**

Visit our corporate website at **www.cengage.com**

Notice to the Reader

Printed in the United States of America
5 6 7 8 9   15 14 13 12 11

FD321

References

Appendices

Responding in a warm, loving, and responsive manner to a crying infant or playing patty-cake with a young toddler both exemplify ways that caregivers and families promote healthy brain development. In fact, recent research on brain development emphasizes the importance of the environment and relationships during the child's first three years of life (Shore, 1997). With this in mind, *Making Sounds, Making Music, and Many Other Activities for Infants: 7 to 12 Months* was written for you, the caregivers and families. The ultimate goal of this book is to assist in promoting healthy development of our youngest children. Thus, it should be part of all parents' and caregivers' libraries.

The book focuses on the growth of the whole child by including norms for physical, language and communication, cognitive, social, and emotional development. To support, enhance, and promote the child's development in all of these areas, this unique book includes specially designed activities for infants. Note that the book has several sections. The first section includes information for understanding, assessing, and promoting development, as well as suggestions for interacting with young children. The next sections include innovative activities to promote development for infants. The last section includes references for the material cited in the text. The appendices are a rich resource including, but not limited to, lists of recipes, songs, finger plays, chants, and books. They also contain a list of toys and equipment, as well as criteria for making selections.

To assist you, the experiences are grouped by age ranges and developmental areas. Each of these activities is designed to illustrate the connection between a broad area of development and specific goals for children. For example, physical development may be the primary area and eye-hand coordination may be one specific goal. The materials, preparation, and nurturing strategies for the activities are designed for easy and effective implementation. Moreover, variations and additional information have been incorporated to enrich the experience for both you and the child. Highlighting Development boxes provide valuable information for fostering an understanding of young children's development. Collectively, the information and experiences provided in this book will enhance your ability to meet the developmental needs of infants, fostering optimal development of the whole child. Furthermore, these early experiences will create a strong foundation for children's subsequent thinking, interacting with others, and learning.

ONLINE RESOURCES™

The Online Resources™ to accompany *Making Sounds, Making Music, and Many Other Activities for Infants: 7 to 12 Months* is your link to early childhood education on the Internet. The Online Resources™ contains many features to help focus your understanding of the learning and teaching process.

♡ Sample Activities and Preface
♡ Developmental Milestones
♡ Books for Infants
♡ Criteria for Selecting Materials and Equipment for Children
♡ Materials and Equipment for Promoting Optimal Development
♡ Favorite Finger Plays, Nursery Rhymes, and Chants
♡ Songs
♡ Rhythm Instruments
♡ Resources Related to Infants
♡ Developmental Checklist
♡ Anecdotal Record
♡ Panel Documentation
♡ Lesson Plan
♡ Daily Communications
♡ A Summarized list of Web links is provided for your reference.
♡ On-line Early Education Survey – This survey gives you the opportunity to let us know what features you want to see improved on the Online Resources™.

The authors and Delmar Cengage Learning make every effort to ensure that all Internet resources are accurate at the time of printing. However, due to the fluid, time-sensitive nature of the Internet, we cannot guarantee that all URLs and Web site addresses will remain current for the duration of this edition.

 You can find the Online Resources™ at earlychilded.delmar.com

ACKNOWLEDGMENTS

We would like to thank many people. First, our husbands, Dr. James Herr and James Daniel Swim, who supported us during this process.

To our families, who have continuously provided encouragement and facilitated our personal and professional development.

Furthermore, this book would not have been possible without the inspiration of the numerous young children who have touched and influenced our lives in so many meaningful ways. The children we have met in university laboratories and child care settings and their teachers and parents have all demonstrated the importance of the early years of life.

We want to acknowledge the contributions of the numerous colleges, universities, colleagues, and students that have fostered our professional growth and development:

College of William and Mary, Norfolk, Virginia; University of Akron, Ohio; Harvard University, Cambridge, Massachusetts; Purdue University, West Lafayette, Indiana; University of Minnesota, Minneapolis, Minnesota; University of Missouri, Columbia, Missouri; University of Texas, Austin, Texas; and University of Wisconsin-Stout, Menomonie, Wisconsin.

Specifically we would like to thank Carla Ahman, Carol Armga, Michelle Batchelder, Chalandra Bryant, Mary Jane Burson-Polston, Bill Carver, Linda Conner, Kay Cutler, Sandi Dillon, Loraine Dunn, Nancy File, Nancy Hazen-Swann, Debra Hughes, Susan Jacquet, Elizabeth Johnson, Joan Jurich, Susan Kontos, Gary Ladd, Julia Lorenz, Pat Morris, Linda Norton-Smith, Barbara O'Donnel, Diana Peyton, Douglas R. Powell, Kathy Pruesse, Julie Rand, Karin Samii, Jen Shields, Cathy Surra, Adriana Umana, Chris Upchurch, Lisa West, and Rhonda Whitman for their encouragement and support.

Also, special thanks to Carol Hagness, University of Wisconsin-Stout Educational Materials Collection Librarian, and Ann Salt, Children's Librarian at the Menomonie Public Library, who developed the list of books for infants that is located in Appendix A; Erin O'Connor, our editor from Delmar Cengage Learning who provided continuous encouragement, support, and creative ideas; and Deb Hass and Vicki Weber, who typed the manuscript.

The authors and publisher would like to thank the following reviewers for their constructive suggestions and recommendations:

Davia Allen
Western Carolina University
Cullowhee, NC

Alice Beyrent
Hesser College
Manchester, NH

Billie Coffman
Pennsylvania College of Technology
Williamsport, PA

Irene Cook
Taft College Children's Center
Taft, CA

Linda Estes
St. Charles County Community College
St. Peters, MO

Jody Martin
Children's World Learning Centers
Golden, CO

Introduction

Smiling, crying, bicycling with their legs, and laughing at caregivers are all signals infants use to gain and maintain attention. Watching them is exciting. They are amazing. Each infant has an individual style; no two are alike. Differences in temperament are apparent from birth. Some infants are quiet, while others are active. Each is unique. However, all infants grow and develop in predictable patterns, even though the exact rate varies from infant to infant.

Development can be defined as change over time. According to Bentzen (2001), development refers to any "change in the structure, thought, or behavior of an individual that comes from biological and environmental influences" (p. 15). Human development occurs in two distinct patterns. First, development proceeds from the top of the body to the bottom. For example, control of the head develops before control of the torso or the legs. The second pattern is for development to proceed from the center of the body outward. To illustrate, the arm muscles develop before those of the hands or fingers.

UNDERSTANDING THEORIES OF DEVELOPMENT

Searching the literature, you will find numerous beliefs about or theories of child growth and development. Some beliefs are in direct opposition to each other. There are theories that state children are biologically programmed at birth. These theories purport that children develop according to their own individual timetable, regardless of environmental influences. In contrast, there are nurture-based theories that emphasize the importance of environmental factors. These theories assume that children enter the world as blank slates. According to these theories, the children's environment is instrumental in molding their abilities. A third set of theories incorporates aspects from both of these two extremes, nature and nurture. These interactional theories are based on the premise that biology and environment work in concert to account for children's development.

While reading this book, you will note that it celebrates interactional theories. Current research on brain development supports the belief that human development hinges on the dynamic interplay between nature and nurture (Shore, 1997). At birth, the development of the child's brain is unfinished. Through early experiences, the brain matures and connections are made for wiring its various parts. Repeated experiences result in the wiring becoming permanent, thereby creating the foundation for the brain's organization and functioning throughout life.

Your role is critical because early experiences significantly affect how each child's brain is wired. The child's relationships with parents, caregivers, and significant others will all influence how the brain becomes wired. Therefore, loving encounters and positive social, emotional, language and communication, cognitive, and physical experiences all influence the development of a healthy brain.

However, this influence is far from unidirectional. Children, for example, are born with different temperaments. Research has shown that children's dispositions influence their involvement with both people and materials in their environment. To illustrate, Quincy is a quiet, slow-to-warm-up child. He initially holds back and observes. Moreover, he becomes very distressed in new situations. To prevent Quincy from feeling distressed, his caregivers and parents sometimes respond by minimizing the introduction of new experiences or situations. Consequently, his physical, language and communication, emotional, social, and cognitive development are shaped by his characteristics and his caregivers' and parents' responses to these characteristics.

USING DEVELOPMENTAL NORMS

Research on human development provides evidence that infants and toddlers grow and develop in predictable sequences or patterns. Such predictable, or universal, patterns of development occur in all domains—physical, cognitive, language and communication, social, and emotional. The specific components of these universal patterns are called developmental norms. Norms provide evidence of when a large group of children, on average, accomplishes a given task. Because norms are averages, they must be interpreted with caution. There are differences from child to child in the timing for reaching developmental milestones within one specific domain and across different domains. For example, a child may reach all developmental milestones as expected in the cognitive domain but develop on a later timetable in the language domain. Hence, each child has a unique pattern of timing of growth and development that must be taken into account.

Notwithstanding their limitations, developmental norms are useful to caregivers and parents for three main reasons. First, they allow for judgments and evaluations of the relative normalcy of a child's developmental progression. If a child is lagging behind in one developmental task, generally there should be little concern. But if a child is behind on numerous tasks, human development specialists should be consulted for further evaluations.

Second, developmental norms are useful in making broad generalizations about the timing of particular skills and behaviors. Understanding the child's current level of development in relation to the norms allows predictions about upcoming tasks. For example, a child who can easily find a toy that is partially hidden is ready to begin searching for a toy that is completely out of view.

This knowledge of future development ties into the third reason why developmental norms are helpful. Developmental norms allow caregivers and parents to create and implement experiences that support and enhance the child's current level of development. Following the example just given, an adult playing a hide-and-seek game could begin by partially hiding a toy with a towel and then add the challenge of completely covering the toy.

The following table includes a list of developmental norms for infants and toddlers, highlighting significant tasks. Norms are grouped by areas of development, and within each area the specific tasks have been arranged sequentially. When using this table, please remember that it represents universal patterns of development. You will need to be cognizant of each child's unique patterns.

Developmental Milestones*

PHYSICAL DEVELOPMENT

Birth to Three Months	Four to Six Months	Seven to Nine Months	Ten to Twelve Months	Thirteen to Eighteen Months	Nineteen to Twenty-Four Months	Twenty-Five to Thirty-Six Months
Acts reflexively—sucking, stepping, rooting	Holds cube in hand	Sits independently	Supports entire body weight on legs	Builds tower of two cubes	Walks up stairs independently, one step at a time	Maneuvers around obstacles in a pathway
Swipes at objects in front of body, uncoordinated	Reaches for objects with one hand	Stepping reflex returns, so that child bounces when held on a surface in a standing position	Walks when hands are held	Turns the pages of a cardboard book two or three at a time	Jumps in place	Runs in a more adult-like fashion; knees are slightly bent, arms move in the opposite direction
Holds head erect and steady when lying on stomach	Rolls from back to side	Leans over and reaches when in a sitting position	Cruises along furniture or steady objects	Scribbles vigorously	Kicks a ball	Walks down stairs independently
Lifts head and shoulders	Reaches for objects in front of body, coordinated	Gets on hands and knees but may fall forward	Stands independently	Walks proficiently	Runs in a modified fashion	Marches to music
Rolls from side to back	Sits with support	Crawls	Walks independently	Walks while carrying or pulling a toy	Shows a decided preference for one hand	Uses feet to propel wheeled riding toys
Follow moving objects with eyes	Transfers objects from hand to hand	Pulls to standing position	Crawls up stairs or steps	Walks up stairs with assistance	Completes a three-piece puzzle with knobs	Rides a tricycle
	Grabs objects with either hand	Claps hands together	Voluntarily releases objects held in hands		Builds a tower of six cubes	Usually uses whole arm movements to paint or color
	Sits in tripod position using arms for support	Stands with adult's assistance	Has good balance when sitting; can shift positions without falling			Throws ball forward, where intended
		Learns pincer grasp, using thumb with forefinger to pick up objects	Takes off shoes and socks			Builds tower using eight or more blocks
		Uses finger and thumb to pick up objects				Imitates drawing circles and vertical and horizontal lines
		Brings objects together with banging noises				Turns pages in book one by one
						Fingers work together to scoop up small objects
						Strings large beads on a shoelace

*The developmental milestones listed are based on universal patterns of when various traits emerge. Because each child is unique certain traits may develop at an earlier or later age.

Developmental Milestones* (continued)

LANGUAGE AND COMMUNICATION DEVELOPMENT

Birth to Three Months	Four to Six Months	Seven to Nine Months	Ten to Twelve Months	Thirteen to Eighteen Months	Nineteen to Twenty-Four Months	Twenty-Five to Thirty-Six Months
Communicates with cries, grunts, and facial expressions	Babbles spontaneously	Varies babble in loudness, pitch, and rhythm	Uses preverbal gestures to influence the behavior of others	Has expressive vocabulary of 10 to 20 words	Continues using telegraphic speech	Continues using telegraphic speech combining three or four words
Prefers human voices	Acquires sounds of native language in babble	Adds *d*, *t*, *n*, and *w* to repertoire of babbling sounds	Demonstrates word comprehension skills	Engages in "jargon talk"	Able to combine three words	Speaks in complete sentences following word order of native language
Coos	Canonical, systematic consonant–vowel pairings; babbling occurs	Produces gestures to communicate, often by pointing	Waves good-bye	Engages in telegraphic speech by combining two words together	Talks, 25 percent of words being understandable	Displays effective conversational skills
Laughs	Participates in interactive games initiated by adults	May say *mama* or *dada* but does not connect words with parents	Speaks recognizable first word	Experiences a burst of language development	Refers to self by name	Refers to self as *me* or *I* rather than by name
Smiles and coos to initiate and sustain interactions with caregiver	Takes turns while interacting		Initiates familiar games with adults	Comprehends approximately 50 words	Joins three or four words into a sentence	Talks about objects and events not immediately present
					Comprehends approximately 300 words	Uses grammatical markers and some plurals
					Expressive language includes a vocabulary of approximately 250 words	Vocabulary increases rapidly, up to 300 words
						Enjoys being read to if allowed to participate by pointing, talking, and turning pages

*The developmental milestones listed are based on universal patterns of when various traits emerge. Because each child is unique certain traits may develop at an earlier or later age.

Developmental Milestones * (continued)

Birth to Three Months	Four to Six Months	Seven to Nine Months	Ten to Twelve Months	Thirteen to Eighteen Months	Nineteen to Twenty-Four Months	Twenty-Five to Thirty-Six Months
Cries for assistance	Recognizes people by their voice	Enjoys looking at books with familiar objects	Solves sensorimotor problems by deliberately using schemas, such as shaking a container to empty its contents	Explores properties of objects by acting on them in novel ways	Points to and identifies objects on request, such as when reading a book, touring, etc.	Uses objects for purposes other than intended
Acts reflexively	Enjoys repeating acts, such as shaking a rattle, that produce results in the external world	Distinguishes familiar from unfamiliar faces	Points to body parts upon request	Solves problems through trial and error	Sorts by shapes and colors	Uses private speech while working
Prefers to look at patterned objects, bull's-eye, horizontal stripes, and the human face	Searches with eyes for source of sounds	Engages in goal-directed behavior	Drops toys intentionally and repeatedly looks in the direction of the fallen object	Experiments with cause-and-effect relationships such as turning on televisions, banging on drums, etc.	Recognizes self in photographs and mirror	Classifies objects based on one dimension, such as toy cars versus blocks
Imitates adults' facial expressions	Enjoys watching hands and feet	Anticipates events	Waves good-bye	Plays body identification games	Demonstrates deferred imitation	Follows two-step directions
Searches with eyes for sources of sounds	Searches for a partially hidden object	Finds objects that are totally hidden	Shows evidence of stronger memory capabilities	Imitates novel behaviors of others	Engages in functional play	Concentrates or attends to self-selected activities for longer periods of time
Begins to recognize familiar people at a distance	Uses toys in a purposeful manner	Imitates behaviors that are slightly different than those usually performed	Follows simple, one-step directions	Identifies family members in photographs	Finds objects that have been moved while out of sight	Points to and labels objects spontaneously, such as when reading a book
Discovers and repeats bodily actions such as sucking, swiping, and grasping	Imitates simple actions	Begins to show interest in filling and dumping containers	Categorizes objects by appearance		Solves problems with internal representation	Coordinates pretend play with other children
Discovers hands and feet as extension of self	Explores toys using existing schemas such as sucking, banging, grasping, shaking, etc.		Looks for objects hidden in a second location		Categorizes self and others by gender, race, hair color, etc.	Gains a nominal sense of numbers through counting and labeling objects in a set
						Begins developing concepts about opposites such as big and small, tall and short, in and out
						Begins developing concepts about time such as today, tomorrow, and yesterday

*The developmental milestones listed are based on universal patterns of when various traits emerge. Because each child is unique certain traits may develop at an earlier or later age.

Developmental Milestones * (continued)

Birth to Three Months	Four to Six Months	Seven to Nine Months	Ten to Twelve Months	Thirteen to Eighteen Months	Nineteen to Twenty-Four Months	Twenty-Five to Thirty-Six Months
Turns head toward a speaking voice	Seeks out adults for play by crying, cooing, or smiling	Becomes upset when separated from a favorite adult	Shows a decided preference for one or two caregivers	Demands personal attention	Shows enthusiasm for company of others	Observes others to see how they do things
Recognizes primary caregiver	Responds with entire body to familiar face by looking at the person, smiling, kicking legs, and waving arms	Acts deliberately to maintain the presence of a favorite adult by clinging or crying	Plays parallel to other children	Imitates behaviors of others	Views the world only from own, egocentric perspective	Engages primarily in solitary or parallel play
Bonds to primary caregiver			Enjoys playing with siblings	Becomes increasingly aware of the self as a separate being	Plays contently alone or near adults	Sometimes offers toys to other children
Finds comfort in the human face		Uses adults as a base for exploration, typically	Begins asserting self	Shares affection with people other than primary caregiver	Engages in functional play	Begins to play cooperatively with other children
Displays a social smile	Participates actively in interactions with others by vocalizing in response to adult speech	Looks to others who are exhibiting signs of distress	Begins developing a sense of humor	Shows ownership of possessions	Defends possessions	Engages in sociodramatic play
Is quieted by a voice	Smiles at familiar faces and stares solemnly at strangers	Enjoys observing and interacting briefly with other children	Develops a sense of self-identity through the identification of body parts	Begins developing a view of self as autonomous when completing tasks independently	Recognizes self in photographs or mirrors	Wants to do things independently
Begins to differentiate self from caregiver	Distinguishes between familar and unfamiliar adults and surroundings	Likes to play and responds to games such as patty-cake and peekaboo	Begins distinguishing boys from girls		Refers to self with pronouns such as I or me	Asserts independence by using "no" a lot
		Engages in solitary play			Categorizes people by using salient characteristics such as race or hair color	Develops a rudimentary awareness that others have wants or feelings that may be different than their own
		Develops preferences for particular people and objects			Shows less fear of strangers	Makes demands of or "bosses" parents, guardians, and caregivers
		Shows distress when in the presence of a stranger				Uses physical aggression less and uses words to solve problems
						Engages in gender steriotypical behavior

*The developmental milestones listed are based on universal patterns of when various traits emerge. Because each child is unique certain traits may develop at an earlier or later age.

Developmental Milestones* (continued)

Birth to Three Months	Four to Six Months	Seven to Nine Months	Ten to Twelve Months	Thirteen to Eighteen Months	Nineteen to Twenty-Four Months	Twenty-Five to Thirty-Six Months
Feels and expresses three basic emotions: interest, distress, and disgust	Expresses delight	Responds to social events by using the face, gaze, voice, and posture to form coherent emotional patterns	Continues to exhibit delight, happiness, discomfort, anger, and sadness	Exhibits autonomy by frequently saying "no"	Expresses affection to others spontaneously	Experiences increase in number of fears
Cries to signal a need	Responds to the emotions of caregivers	Expresses fear and anger more often	Expresses anger when goals are blocked	Labels several emotions	Acts to comfort others in distress	Begins to understand the consequences of basic emotions
Quiets in response to being held, typically	Begins to distinguish familiar from unfamiliar people	Begins to regulate emotions through moving into or out of experiences	Expresses anger at the source of frustration	Connects feelings with social behaviors	Shows the emotions of pride and embarrassment	Learns skills for coping with strong emotions
Feels and expresses enjoyment	Shows a preference for being held by a familiar person	Begins to detect the meaning of others' emotional expressions	Begins to show compliance to caregivers' requests	Begins to understand complicated patterns of behavior	Uses emotion words spontaneously in conversations or play	Seeks to communicate more feelings with specific words
Shares a social smile	Begins to assist with holding a bottle	Looks to others for cues on how to react	Often objects to having playtime stopped	Demonstrates the ability to communicate needs	Begins to show sympathy to another child or adult	Shows signs of empathy and caring
Reads and distinguishes adults' facial expressions	Expresses happiness selectively by laughing and smiling more with familiar people	Shows fear of strangers	Begins eating with a spoon	May say "no" to something they want	Becomes easily hurt by criticism	Loses control of emotions and throws temper tantrums
Begins to self-regulate emotional expressions			Assists in dressing and undressing	May lose emotional control and have temper tantrums	Experiences a temper tantrum when goals are blocked, on occasion	Able to recover from temper tantrums
Laughs aloud			Acts in loving, caring ways toward dolls or stuffed animals, typically	Shows self-conscious emotions such as shame, guilt, and shyness	Associates facial expressions with simple emotional labels	Enjoys helping with chores such as cleaning up toys or carrying grocery bags
Quiets self by using techniques such as sucking a thumb or pacifier			Feeds self a complete meal when served finger foods	Becomes frustrated easily		Begins to show signs of being ready for toileting
			Claps when successfully completes a task			Desires that routines be carried out exactly as has been done in the past

*The developmental milestones listed are based on universal patterns of when various traits emerge. Because each child is unique certain traits may develop at an earlier or later age.

ASSESSING DEVELOPMENT

"All children have the potential, albeit in different ways, to learn and to develop their own ideas, theories, and strategies. All children also have the right to be supported in these endeavors by adults. Teachers and parents, therefore, should observe and listen to them" (Gandini & Goldhaber, 2001, p. 125).

Assessment is the process of observing, listening, recording, and documenting behavior in order to make decisions about a child's developmental and, thus, educational needs. This process is applicable for an individual child, a small group, or an entire group of children. Your observation skills are the main tools needed for assessing development. By observing and listening, you will discover much about children's needs, interests, and abilities.

This is a simple process. Your eyes and ears are like a video camera capturing children's behaviors, language, attitudes, and preferences. Most of the time you should be examining the children's abilities on worthy and meaningful tasks that you have created. Thus, your assessments will be directly tied to the curriculum that you have planned and implemented. For example, you do this when interacting with an infant or when assisting a toddler who is busy "working" at an experience. In other words, this is a spontaneous process that is continuously occurring. Authentic assessment requires your focused attention and some additional time for documenting your observation. To assist you in this process, a checklist has been included in Appendix H. If you are caring for more than one child, reproduce a copy for each. Appendix I is a form for recording anecdotal records. This form will allow you to document behaviors and incidents not represented on the checklist.

You can also record the children's performance during an activity, using a camera to document behavior and abilities.

There are several reasons why caregivers and parents need to assess the development of young children. First, assessment tracks growth and development, noting progress and change over time, thereby providing evidence of learning and maturation. Each observation conducted by a parent or caregiver provides a "snapshot" of the child's development. Combining several snapshots over time provides a comprehensive composite of the changes in the child's growth and development. These changes can be in one of three directions. Typically, children's growth and development follow a predictable sequence. That is, infants coo before they babble. Likewise, they produce a social smile before they are able to wave good-bye. Children can also continue working on the same skills. For example, they may spend several weeks or even months working on picking up objects with their thumbs and fingers. Finally, children can regress in their development. Although this happens infrequently, it can occur in times of great stress. For example, a toddler who had demonstrated proficiency at using a spoon at mealtime may revert back to using fingers to eat nonfinger foods.

Second, assessment provides insight to children's styles, interests, and dispositions. This information is invaluable in determining the correct level of responsiveness by parents and caregivers. It is much easier to meet a child's needs when you understand, for example, that the infant has difficulty transitioning from one activity to another. Knowing this assists you in preparing the infant for the next component of your daily routine, such as eating lunch.

Third, assessment data provides you with information regarding the normalcy of children's growth and development. This information directly impacts the experiences you create for the children. You should plan a balance of activities that support, enhance, and foster all areas of development. Some activities should be repetitious and represent developmental tasks that a child has accomplished yet still shows interest in and enjoys. Other activities should be a continuation of developmental tasks that the child is currently mastering. Still other activities should stimulate the child's development by requiring a higher skill level, thereby providing a challenge. At these times, children may need more adult support and assistance for scaffolding their learning as well as building their confidence as competent learners.

Fourth, developmental data must be gathered for effectively communicating the child's development with others. For example, if you are caring for children other than your own, you could discuss their progress with their parents or guardians. Likewise, if you are a parent, you will want to share this information with your child's caregiver, your significant other, or your child's pediatrician. Then, too, you may want to compile a portfolio or scrapbook containing a developmental checklist, photographs, videotapes, artwork, and other documents representing the child's growth and development.

Finally, assessment must be conducted to ensure that data is gathered for all areas of development. People have different biases and values. As a result, they may overlook or slight one area of development because of selective attention. If all areas are not assessed, experiences, toys, and equipment provided for children may not meet their developmental needs.

To undertake effective assessment, you will want to compile the data you collect into a meaningful form. The format you choose will depend on how you intend to use the data (Helm, Beneke, & Steinheimer, 1998). For example, if you wish to communicate with others about learning that occurred during a specific activity, you could display the artifacts collected, the photographs taken, and the dialogue transcribed while the children were working. If working in an early childhood program, this information could be displayed on a two-dimensional panel (see Appendix J) or a three-dimensional "Look at

What I Did Table." Moreover, to communicate about one child's current level of development, you might want to create a portfolio containing significant artifacts, such as a developmental checklist, anecdotal records, running records, photographs, and videotapes.

RESPECTING INFANTS

Respect. Regard. Honor. Value. These words are seldom used to describe very young children. Yet, these are traits or characteristics that are desired and valued in older children and adults. How better to teach such traits than to model them to infants from the very beginning? Respect must be demonstrated in your behaviors. More importantly, respect for infants must be something that emanates from inside of you. You have to believe that infants are worthy of your time and attention as individuals, because a respectful relationship is vital to all aspects of child development. For example, when infants are respected, they learn to trust that adults can be counted on to meet their needs. This foundation of trust allows them to actively explore their environment during toddlerhood. Hence, trust leads to learning about the world and the toddler's place in it.

It may seem hard to demonstrate respect to infants because we are unaccustomed to thinking about very young children in this manner. However, it is not difficult. Respect means believing in the children's abilities to explore, solve problems, or cause events to happen in their world. It also means setting and enforcing clear boundaries for behavior.

COMMUNICATING WITH INFANTS

Parents and caregivers play a vital role in helping children master communication and language skills. Listen to the infant-directed speech people use while interacting with and speaking to infants. Originally, this speech was referred to as "motherese"; now it is called "parentese." This type of speech involves speaking slowly and exaggerating changes both in intonation and pitch.

When people use parentese while speaking to an infant, the higher pitch and slower pace capture the child's attention. Then, too, the careful enunciation and simplified style and meanings make the speech easier for the child to understand. By emphasizing one word in a sentence, the adult helps to provide a focal point for the child. When speaking parentese, adults consciously reinforce the infant's role in the conversation by encouraging turn taking and responding to the child's utterances. The following example illustrates the components of parentese:

> Caregiver: *"Look at the kitteeee."*
> Infant responds by cooing: *"Ahhhhh."*
> Caregiver: *"The kitty is black."*
> Infant responds by cooing: *"Ahhhh."*

> Caregiver: *"The cat is eating now."*
> Infant responds by cooing: *"Ohhhh."*
> Caregiver: *"Yes, you knew the cat was hungry."*

Common features of parentese are highlighted in the following table:

Common Features of "Parentese"

Producing Sounds
♡ Exaggerates intonation and uses higher pitch
♡ Moves frequently between high and low pitches, occasionally whispers
♡ Enunciates more clearly
♡ Emphasizes one or two words in a sentence
♡ Parrots a child's pronunciation, correct or incorrect

Simplifying Meanings
♡ Substitutes simple words for more complicated ones: moo moo for cow
♡ Uses diminutives: doggy for dog
♡ Labels objects according to simplest category: bird for parrot
♡ Repeats words invented by child: baba for bottle

Modifying Grammar
♡ Simplifies sentences grammatically to use short sentences: daddy go
♡ Uses nouns in lieu of pronouns: mommy helping Jeffrey
♡ Uses plural pronouns, if spoken: We drink our bottle

Interacting with a Child
♡ Focuses on naming objects, sounds, or events in the immediate environment
♡ Asks and answers own questions
♡ Uses questions more than statements or commands
♡ Pauses to allow for turn taking
♡ Repeats own utterances
♡ Responds to the child's utterances through repeating, expanding, and recasting

(Baron, 1992; Snow, 1998; Zigler & Stevenson, 1993)

Once young children begin understanding language, they begin using it. Language comprehension occurs before production. In the beginning, new words emerge slowly, then suddenly there is a burst. Nouns are acquired more rapidly than verbs. Children's first words focus on their body parts, toys, clothing, and words for social interaction such as *bye-bye* and *hello*. After developing and expressing a repertoire of single words, between 18 months and 2 years of age, children begin to combine words to make two-word phrases for communicating.

Kratcoski and Katz (1998) offer some guiding principles that can be used to support the children's language growth including:

♡ Use simple sentences.

♡ Speak slowly and clearly.

♡ Vary your tone/expression to emphasize key words.

♡ Use concrete vocabulary.

♡ Build from the child's utterance/phrase.

♡ Follow the child's topic of interest.

♡ Try to "comment" more than question. (p. 31)

Likewise, you need to:

♡ Provide the child with labels for objects, feelings, ideas, colors, and shapes.

♡ Give the child an opportunity to learn vocabulary in meaningful ways, and provide new objects and experiences to expand the child's language.

♡ Expose the child to a variety of books, catchy rhymes, and music.

♡ Connect the child's actions, ideas, and emotions with words.

♡ Engage in verbal interactions focusing on the child's interest. Prompt the child either by asking questions or creating a situation that requires a response.

♡ Engage the child in problem solving.

♡ Provide toys and household items that stimulate the child to talk.

RESPONDING TO INFANT BEHAVIORAL STATES

An infant's cues are important. Infants experience seven different behavioral states that caregivers need to recognize. Each behavioral state is characterized by differences in facial expressions, muscle tone, and alertness. Following birth, the newborn has irregular states. Predictable patterns, however, emerge within a few weeks. Additionally, newborns spend the majority of their day, between 16 and 20 hours, sleeping. As the baby grows and develops, the amount of sleep time decreases. Accordingly, the amount of time the infant is awake begins increasing. When this occurs, you will need to spend more time interacting with the child. The table above provides valuable information for recognizing the seven behavioral states. Study it carefully to be able to respond to the infant's cues.

Providing stimulation and the timing of interactions is important. Infants should not be interrupted or stimulated during regular, irregular, or periodic sleep or drowsiness. Rather, caregivers should observe for quiet alert periods. During this state, the infant exhibits a relaxed face and bright, focused eyes that are fully open. The child's activities are slight. Typically, the infant's hands will be open, with arms bent at the elbows and fingers extended.

SOOTHING INFANTS

When infants are crying, the caregiver should respond immediately. This reaction is important because children need to experience predictable and consistent care. Such care results in learning to trust, which is the foundation for later social-emotional development. Furthermore, responding promptly to the cries of infants is vital to the development of language and communica-

INFANT BEHAVIORAL STATES AND APPROPRIATE ADULT RESPONSES

State	Facial Expression	Action	Adult Response
Regular Sleep	Eyes closed and still; face relaxed	Little movement; fingers slightly curled, thumbs extended	Do not disturb
Irregular Sleep	Eyes closed, occasional rapid eye movement; smiles and grimaces	Gentle movement	Do not disturb
Periodic Sleep/ Drowsiness	Alternates between regular and irregular sleep; eyes open and close or remain halfway open; eyes dull/glazed	Less movement than in irregular sleep; hands open and relaxed, fingers extended	Do not disturb; Pick up if drowsiness follows sleeping; do not disturb if drowsiness follows awake periods
Quiet Alert	Bright eyes, fully open; face relaxed; eyes focused	Slight activity; hands open, fingers extended, arms bent at elbow; stares	Talk to infant; present objects; perform any assessment
Waking Activity	Face flushed; less able to focus eyes than in quiet alert state	Extremities and body move; vocalizes, makes noises	Interact with infant; provide basic care
Crying	Red skin; facial grimaces; eyes partially or fully open	Vigorous activity; crying vocalizations; fists are clenched	Pick up immediately; try to identify source of discomfort and remedy it; soothe infant

Adapted from Kostelnik et al. (2002)

tion skills. This teaches children that through communication their needs will be met.

Many caregivers worry that promptly responding to infants' cries will result in spoiling them. Current research suggests this is not true. In fact, some studies found that promptly responding to the cries of very young infants results in less crying at later stages of development (Zigler & Stevenson, 1993). The infants, in essence, have learned to trust that their communication results in signaling their caregivers.

The following table provides suggestions for soothing infants, including reasons for their effectiveness:

Soothing Crying Infants: Techniques and Reasons for Effectiveness

Technique	Reasons for Effectiveness
Lift baby to your shoulder and rock or walk	Provides a combination of physical contact, upright posture, and motion

Technique	Reasons for Effectiveness
Wrap tightly in a blanket	Restricts movement while increasing warmth
Offer a fist or pacifier	Provides pleasurable oral stimulation
Talk softly or provide a rhythmic sound such as a ticking clock or whirling fan	Reminds child of mother's heart-beat heard while in the uterus
Provide gentle rhythmic motions such as a short walk in a stroller or a ride in a swing	Lulls an infant to sleep
Massage the infant's body with continuous, gentle strokes	Relaxes the infant's muscles

INTERPRETING NONVERBAL CUES

Developing a social relationship with children is paramount and dependent on your ability to interpret their behaviors. This requires careful observation. You will study children's nonverbal behavioral cues. To illustrate, if the child is looking at you face-to-face, this behavior can be interpreted as being fully engaged. When this occurs, continue the interaction. However, if the child lowers the head, it is time to stop. The following table will provide you with some ways to interpret infants' behaviors and facial expressions:

Infant Gaze and Social Meaning to Caregivers

Position and Expression	Typical Interpretation
Face-to-face, sober	Fully engaged, intent
Face-to-face, smiling	Pleased, interested
Head turned slightly away	Maintaining interest; interaction too fast or too slow
Complete head rotation	Uninterested; stop for a while
Head lowered	Stop
Rapid head rotation	Dislikes something
Glances away, tilts head up; partial head aversion	Stop or change strategy
Head lowered, body limp	Has given up fighting off overstimulation

Source: Kostelnik et al. (2002)

If you fail to recognize the child's cues, the infant may become overstimulated. Overstimulation can result from interactions that are too intense. Noises or voices that are too loud can also contribute to overstimulation. When overstimulation occurs, infants protect themselves by changing from one state to another. Because there can be a rapid fluctuation between states, the goodness of fit between the child's state, the caregiver, and the environment is important. When children signal changes in state, alter your behavior immediately. Cease the interaction even without completing the activity. Of course, when the child signals readiness, the activity can be reintroduced.

APPLYING THIS BOOK

This book can be a wonderful companion when working with infants. To use it effectively, you will need to begin by reviewing the developmental norms and assessments. After this, you can use the checklist in Appendix I to begin gathering and documenting data. Once you have collected this developmental data, evaluate it to determine each child's needs, interests, and abilities. At this point, you are ready to begin searching for activities in this book that provide a balance of experiences to support, enhance, and foster all developmental areas.

When undertaking this process, you will need to narrow your selection of activities to prevent overstimulating the child(ren) in your care. This minimizes your preparation time and the amount of materials and equipment required; hence, you will have more energy to expend while interacting with the child(ren) in your care.

While working with infants, questions often arise. To support you, a list of resources related to infants has been included in Appendix G. You may discover these resources can be very useful in supporting your role as a caregiver.

We hope you enjoy reading and implementing the activities in this book as much as we did developing them. We leave you with this thought:

For a baby, those early weeks and months of growth, understanding, and reasoning can never be brought back to do over again. This is not the rehearsal. This is the main show. (Irving Harris)

Promoting Optimal Development in Infants

SEVEN to NINE MONTHS

TEN to TWELVE MONTHS

PHYSICAL

LANGUAGE & COMMUNICATION

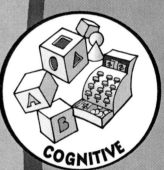

COGNITIVE

SOCIAL

EMOTIONAL

Physical Development

♡

SEVEN to NINE MONTHS

Clapping

PHYSICAL

Child's Developmental Goals

✓ To practice clapping hands
✓ To practice coordinating hand movements

MATERIALS:

None

PREPARATION:

♡ Observe the child's level of alertness.

NURTURING STRATEGIES:

1. If the child is alert, this activity can be introduced any time throughout the day. It is especially good to do after diapering.

2. While you are changing the diaper, gain the infant's attention by slowly singing:

   ♫ Clap, clap, clap your hands
   ♫ Clap your hands together.
   ♫ Clap, clap, clap your hands
   ♫ Clap your hands together.

3. Reinforcing your words with actions may assist the child in developing association skills. Infants this age can easily imitate your behaviors when they are slightly different than usually performed. If your modeling fails to result in imitation, you can physically move the infant's hand for encouragement while singing the song.

4. Infants show their enjoyment through clapping. Therefore, they continue smiling and clapping even when the song is over.

5. Continue singing the song as long as the infant shows interest by smiling and maintaining eye contact.

☀ Highlighting Development

Clapping is a difficult skill for infants to master because it requires eye-hand coordination and bilateral coordination of arms and hands. Bilateral coordination is the ability of infants to cross the midline of their bodies with their hands. Infants first demonstrate this ability when they transfer objects from one hand to the other around four to six months of age. To be successful at clapping, several muscles must work together. Moreover, the timing of the movements is important in order for the hands to meet.

VARIATION:

♡ Recite your favorite nursery rhyme, sharing your enthusiasm and clapping to the rhythm.

ADDITIONAL INFORMATION:

♡ Infants at this stage of development are unable to maintain a steady rhythm because of a lack of coordination. Continued exposure to this type of activity fosters development.

Splashing

Child's Developmental Goals

✓ To refine eye-hand coordination skills

✓ To continue developing balance by sitting unassisted

MATERIALS:

❏ Warm water

❏ Large, nonbreakable mixing bowl

❏ Vinyl tablecloth

PREPARATION:

♡ Exercise caution when selecting an area for this experience. To protect the flooring, spread out a vinyl tablecloth.

♡ Fill a bowl with warm water and place it on the middle of the tablecloth.

♡ If the room is warm and not drafty, remove the infant's outer clothing. However, if the room is drafty or cool, put a large, waterproof bib on the infant and roll up his sleeves, if necessary.

NURTURING STRATEGIES:

1. Sit the infant on the mat, close to the bowl.
2. Gain the infant's attention by moving the water with your hand while saying:
   "Joben, here is some warm water. Touch it! Feel it!"
   "Splash like me."
3. Reinforcing your words with actions may be necessary. If needed, using your wet hand, touch the child's hand and say:
   "Joben, see. It is warm water."
   If the child does touch the water, gently guide the infant's hand to the bowl while saying:
   "Joben, let's splash together."

4. Providing positive reinforcement may encourage the child to repeat the behavior. Say, for example:
   "Joben, you are splashing the water."
   "What a smile! You must like splashing."

☼ Highlighting Development

Toward the end of this developmental stage, infants have made milestones in motor development. They will be able to sit alone steadily, raise themselves to a sitting position, stand up by furniture, and cruise along the crib rail. They also are able to successfully reach and grasp with their hands. Observe them. They can transfer objects from one hand to another (Black & Puckett, 1996). Even though they use both hands, they are developing a preference for one hand. Dominance of one side of the body usually is not stable until about 24 months of age.

VARIATIONS:

♡ Repeat this activity outside if weather permits.

♡ Add one tool to the bowl such as a measuring cup.

ADDITIONAL INFORMATION:

♡ Periodically check the water to make sure it is the right temperature. If necessary, add warm water.

 To prevent accidentally burning the child's hand, test the water in the bowl. It should be about the temperature of a warmed bottle.

Walking Together

Child's Developmental Goals

✓ To practice the stepping reflex

✓ To develop balancing skills

MATERIALS:

None

PREPARATION:

♡ To reduce safety hazards, clear pathways.

NURTURING STRATEGIES:

1. Respond to the infant's desire to walk. The infant, for example, may be attempting unsuccessfully to walk. Observe and intervene before the infant becomes frustrated.

2. Provide positive reinforcement by commenting to the child, for example:
   "Jamila, you are working hard."
   "Walking takes practice."
   "Good work. You're getting it!"

3. Volunteer to assist the infant. To illustrate, say:
   "Jamila, can I help you walk?"
   "Can we walk together?"

4. If the child responds positively to your question, hold out your hands while saying:
   "Jamila, take my hands. Let's practice walking together."

5. If the infant responds negatively to your question, allow independent work while continuing to provide positive reinforcement (see step 2).

6. If a child becomes distressed because of unsuccessful attempts while refusing your assistance, it is time to stop the activity. Say to the infant, for example:
   "Jamila, walking is hard. We'll practice again later."

☼ Highlighting Development

What motivates infants to stand is not fully understood. One of their motivations may be to obtain attractive objects at eye level. The stepping reflex is present at birth but vanishes in a few days or weeks. At about seven months of age, standing is really a reflex stiffening of the body. Usually infants begin standing by pulling themselves up. Typically, infants enjoy standing and walking with assistance. As a result, these actions are repeated. They also gain skill in cruising by holding on to furniture and walking around. Before infants can walk, they need to master standing in an erect position. Infants also need to have enough confidence to let go and stand without support (Snow, 1998).

VARIATION:

♡ Assist the infant in walking whenever you need her to change locations. Your physical support will guide her direction.

ADDITIONAL INFORMATION:

♡ Infants have different temperaments. Some infants will easily give up on a task while others will continue to the point of becoming distressed. Your knowledge of the child will assist you in providing the right amount of reinforcement and in intervening at the proper time.

Stepping Up

Child's Developmental Goals

✓ To practice the stepping reflex

✓ To practice balancing skills

MATERIALS:

❑ Flat surface, such as floor

PREPARATION:

♡ Select an area that can be constantly supervised. Make sure you can monitor other children who may be present.

♡ Clear this area of toys and other obstacles that could present a safety hazard.

NURTURING STRATEGIES:

1. While carrying the infant to the cleared area, talk about what is going to happen. For example, comment:

   "Liam, let's work over here. You can stand up on the floor."

2. Sit down, placing your legs in front of your body. Shape them in a "V." To visually connect with the infant, stand the child between your legs facing you.

3. Because the standing position practices a reflex, the child's legs will begin to move as soon as the feet touch the floor.

4. Hold the infant securely under the arms. Avoid holding the child's hands or arms, which could result in an injury to his shoulder if balance is lost.

5. Be cautioned: Infants are typically "wild" during this activity. They become excited by the movements and then the jumping or dancing increases.

6. Providing positive reinforcement may be unnecessary because of the intense pleasure of the activity. However, commenting on the child's expressions will foster emotional development. Say, for example:

   "Liam, what a laugh! You like moving your legs."
   "You are really enjoying this activity."

☀ Highlighting Development

When infants practice the stepping reflex, their knees and elbows may produce crackling sounds. This noise signals how loosely supported the joints are at this period of development. This noise will disappear as the muscles become stronger.

VARIATION:

♡ Hold the infant in a standing position on your legs while you are sitting on a chair.

ADDITIONAL INFORMATION:

♡ In preparation for walking, the stepping reflex returns. The reflex will develop from a jumping motion such as bending and straightening knees at the same time to a dancing motion, alternatively lifting and placing the feet. Walking with assistance can begin after the infant's reflex has reached the "dancing" stage of development.

Come and Get It

PHYSICAL

7 to 9 months

Child's Developmental Goals

✓ To strengthen and coordinate muscles by developing crawling skills

✓ To move one's body to obtain a desired object

MATERIALS:

❑ Favorite stuffed infant toy

❑ Blanket

PREPARATION:

♡ Select and clear an area that you can constantly supervise. Spread out the blanket in the area.

♡ Place the favorite toy near the edge of the blanket.

NURTURING STRATEGIES:

1. While carrying the infant to the blanket, talk about the activity. To illustrate, say:
   "Bria, you can practice crawling on this blanket. See if you can crawl over to the bunny."

2. Lay the infant facedown on the blanket.

3. Move over by the infant toy. Gain the infant's attention by moving the toy and saying:
   "Bria, crawl over here. Come get the bunny."

4. Providing positive reinforcement may encourage the infant to continue the desired behaviors. Comments might include:
   "Bria, you are crawling. Keep going."
   "You are almost there."
   "Come get the bunny."

5. Encourage the infant to explore the toy once it is reached. Say, for example:
   "Bria, shake it."
   "Touch it. Use your fingers."

☀ Highlighting Development

Frequently, the definitions of crawling and creeping in common usage are reversed. Crawling occurs when the infant's abdomen is on the ground. Infants use the hands to slide the body forward or backward. When crawling, their legs usually drag behind. Creeping differs. As muscle strength increases in the legs, the child advances toward creeping (Snow, 1998; Bukato & Daehler, 1995). When infants can get up on bent knees and elbows, they are able to creep. Most infants creep backward before they creep forward. When infants first learn to creep, they raise up on their hands and knees and rock back and forth (Herr, 1998). During this process, they often lose their balance, falling forward or backward.

VARIATION:

♡ Encourage the infant to crawl to you.

ADDITIONAL INFORMATION:

♡ Use your knowledge of each child's crawling abilities in deciding how far away to place the toy.

 Whenever pillows or blankets are used, constant supervision is necessary to prevent the possibility of suffocation.

Ramping It

Child's Developmental Goals

✓ To practice creeping skills

✓ To refine balancing skills

MATERIALS:

❑ Foam ramp

❑ Foam pads or mats

❑ Interesting infant toys that roll

PREPARATION:

♡ Select an area that you can constantly supervise.

♡ Arrange the foam ramp so that it is surrounded by the other mats. Carefully check that a safe fall zone has been created.

♡ Place the infant toy at the top of the ramp.

NURTURING STRATEGIES:

1. Allow the infant to select this activity. As soon as an infant creeps near the area, provide assistance or support.

2. Describe the activity for the infant. For example, say:
   "Toshi, creep to the top of the ramp."
   "Creep up the ramp and get the ball."

3. Providing positive reinforcement may result in the infant continuing the desired behaviors. Comments might include:
   "Toshi, you are working hard."
   "Keep creeping. You are almost to the top."
   "Toshi, you did it. You got the ball."

☀ Highlighting Development

At this stage of development, children move from one place to another in a variety of ways. Some children crawl by pulling themselves on their bellies; some infants creep on their hands and knees; still others use their hands and feet. Hitching is another movement infants make, occurring after they are able to sit without support. By moving their arms and legs, infants will slide their buttocks across the floor (Herr, 1998).

VARIATION:

♡ Encourage the infant to roll the toys down the ramp.

ADDITIONAL INFORMATION:

♡ After infants can roll onto their stomach and sit alone, crawling will appear.

♡ Locomotion against gravity is a much more difficult task. Therefore, introduce this activity only after the child has experienced some success creeping.

 For safety reasons, never leave an infant unattended during this activity.

Pulling It Around

PHYSICAL

7 to 9 months

Child's Developmental Goals

✓ To develop a pincer grasp

✓ To refine eye-hand coordination skills

MATERIALS:

❑ 2 pull toys

PREPARATION:

♡ Clear a space for this activity in a noncarpeted area so that the toys will easily roll.

♡ Place the pull toys in an open area of the identified space.

NURTURING STRATEGIES:

1. While carrying the infant to the area, talk about the upcoming activity. Say, for example:
   "Darlene, I have a toy for you to play with. You pull the string and it moves."

2. Sit the infant on the floor.

3. Encourage the child to grasp the string.
   To illustrate, say:
   "Darlene, pick up the string."

4. Observe how the infant picks up the string. Did she use a pincer grasp?
   If so, reinforce that behavior by saying:
   "Wow. You used your thumb."
   If the child has not demonstrated the pincer grasp, encourage that behavior by commenting:
   "Use your thumb and finger. Let me show you."

5. Reinforcing your words with actions may be necessary. If so, model the pincer grasp while explaining:
   "Watch me. Look, Darlene. I'm picking up the string with my thumb and finger."

6. Once the infant has picked up the string, observe her actions and exploration of the toy.

7. Encourage the infant to move the pull toy by suggesting:
   "Darlene, move your hand."
   "Pull the string."

8. Reinforce the infant's play with the toy.
   To illustrate, say:
   "Darlene, look at the wheels move."
   "You are pulling the toy."

☀ Highlighting Development

Infants are learning to use just their hands. Observe. At this stage of development, waving is becoming more sophisticated. They can wave now by turning their hand and wrist. Up to this point, waving occurred by moving the entire arm.

VARIATION:

♡ Encourage the infant to pull the toy while crawling. When the child has mastered walking, introduce the pull toy again.

ADDITIONAL INFORMATION:

♡ Infants are gaining control of their separate fingers. This allows them to point as well as perform a pincer grasp.

♡ To encourage forward movement, put toys just beyond arm's reach in front of crawlers.

Language and Communication Development

SEVEN to NINE MONTHS

Making Sounds

7 to 9 months

Child's Developmental Goals

✓ To practice producing babbling sounds
✓ To add new sounds to babbling

MATERIALS:

None

PREPARATION:

♡ Closely observe the infant's babbling. Conduct an assessment by asking yourself, "What sounds am I hearing?"

NURTURING STRATEGIES:

1. Join in a conversation with the infant. To do this, wait until the infant pauses, then imitate the same sounds the child was producing.
2. When your turn to talk arrives again in the conversation, introduce one new sound for infant to imitate. For example, say:
   "Wo wo wo."
   "Nu nu nu."
3. Providing positive reinforcement may result in the infant repeatedly making the new sound. For example, say:
   "You can do it. Wowowowowo. Keep trying."
   "That's right. Nununu. You've got it."
4. Listen. If the infant repeats your sounds, echo them again.

☀ Highlighting Development

Babbling begins at about four months of age and may continue into the second year. During babbling, the infant will keep repeating the same vowels and consonants. However, the pitch will change from high to low. Babbling will progress from simple to complex. Infants typically add the sounds of *d*, *t*, *n*, and *w* to their babbling at about seven months (Feldman, 1998).

At seven or eight months of age, babies around the world typically make four basic sounds: "ba ba," "da da," "ma ma," and "wa wa." These sounds are considered a universal first step toward speaking.

VARIATION:

♡ To provide a challenge, add two new sounds at once.

ADDITIONAL INFORMATION:

♡ Try to reduce interference from other sources of stimulation such as the television or stereo while verbally encouraging the child to babble.
♡ Communicating with children is important. They learn they are loved and worthwhile through praise and smiles from caregivers.

Talking to Toys

Child's Developmental Goals

✓ To practice producing babbling sounds

✓ To listen to native language patterns

MATERIALS:

❑ 2 or 3 stuffed animal toys

PREPARATION:

♡ Select an area that can be constantly supervised. Clear this area and lay out the toys you gathered for the activity.

NURTURING STRATEGIES:

1. If the infant is unable to crawl, carry the child to the carpeted area. If the infant can crawl, encourage the child to do so. One way to do this is to hold up one of the toys while commenting:
   "Edwardo, come and get the pig. The pig wants to play."
   "Here is your favorite toy. It is a bear."
2. Observe the infant interacting with or exploring with the toy.
3. Reinforce the infant's spontaneous babbles. Comments might include:
   "Edwardo, you are talking to the bear."
   "Tell the pig more about that."

 Highlighting Development

While babbling, infants will begin to experiment with both rhythm and loudness. Often the sound of the infant's changing voice will attract your attention. Providing reinforcement for these variations may result in more experimentation.

VARIATION:

♡ Move the infant toy while "talking" for it.

ADDITIONAL INFORMATION:

♡ For some children, the act of remembering will give them pleasure. When they recognize a favorite toy, they will squeal with delight and make small gurgling sounds of joy.

♡ For behaviors you want infants to repeat, praise them. Use eye contact and speak in a soft voice.

♡ Use the "feeding in" technique while interacting with the child. This technique involves introducing simple words to describe the child's actions. To illustrate, you might say:
   "Edwardo, you are banging the block."

7 to 9 months

Looking at Books

7 to 9 months

Child's Developmental Goals

✓ To listen to native language patterns

✓ To engage in conversational turn taking

MATERIALS:

❏ 3 to 4 cardboard books with simple pictures

PREPARATION:

♡ Select an area for interaction that will not distract the infant. Set the books upright and slightly open on the floor in that area.

NURTURING STRATEGIES:

1. When an infant crawls over to the books, move closer to the child.
2. Observe the infant's interaction with the book.
3. Offer to read the book to the infant by asking, for example:
   "Lucinda, would you like me to read the book?"
   "May I read to you?"
4. If the infant shows interest, begin reading the book. If the infant does not appear interested, continue to observe her.
5. Verbally label each picture while pointing to it.
6. While reading the book, periodically ask questions about the pictures to engage the infant in conversation. Pause after each question, allowing time for the infant to respond. Then provide positive reinforcement for any vocalizations or gestures.
   For example:
   "Lucinda, what is this?" Pause. "That's right; it is a baby who is eating."
   "Lucinda, what animal is this?" Pause. "Yes, you pointed to the monkey."

☀ Highlighting Development

Children between seven and nine months of age are capable of producing a variety of sounds. Listen. You will hear *m*, *b*, and *p* sounds. They are also beginning to imitate your intonation and speech sounds. Infants must have this understanding before they are able to produce words themselves.

VARIATION:

♡ Provide vinyl or cloth books for the infant to explore unassisted.

ADDITIONAL INFORMATION:

♡ Given their improved fine motor skills, infants at this stage are ready to begin reading books unassisted. Books with thick pages are easier for infants to page through. Children this age often engage in "mouthing" books, so vinyl books are also a good choice because they can be washed or easily sanitized.

Turning Pages

Child's Developmental Goals

✓ To practice producing babbling sounds

✓ To "read" a book by independently turning the pages

MATERIALS:

❑ 2 or 3 books

PREPARATION:

♡ Prop the books upright and slightly open on the floor to gain the infant's attention.

NURTURING STRATEGIES:

1. When the infant crawls near the books, move closer to the child.
2. Observe what the infant does with the book. Note, for example, how he turns the pages or how he verbally labels the pictures. While turning the pages and looking at the pictures, the infant may point and babble.
3. Providing positive reinforcement may encourage repetition of the desired behavior. Reinforce the behaviors that you want to see continued. Say, for example:
   "Isaiah, you are turning the pages by yourself."
4. If a desired behavior was not observed, encouraging the infant may result in the behavior being performed. Suggest, for example:
   "Isaiah, point to the bunny. Talk to the bunny."
5. If the infant attempts or accomplishes the encouraged behavior, provide positive reinforcement by saying, for example:
   "Isaiah, you pointed to the bunny."
   "You are talking to the bunny."

☼ Highlighting Development

According to recent research, the most important year for brain development is the first (Shore, 1997). The results of these studies have major implications for understanding the needs of young children. Talking, singing, cuddling while reading a book, and rocking are all important experiences for infants and toddlers.

VARIATION:

♡ Read the book together. Point to the pictures and verbally label the objects. The infant can also participate by turning the pages and babbling.

ADDITIONAL INFORMATION:

♡ Some books are designed especially for infants such as those in which the next page raises slightly when the top page is turned. This allows the infants to easily grasp and turn the page using their thumb and forefinger, which is called a pincer grasp.

♡ To prevent them from tuning out, infants also need periods of quiet. These times will encourage the infant to look at things and to practice making sounds with their own voices (Abrams & Kaufman 1990).

Reading Nursery Rhymes

7 to 9 months

Child's Developmental Goals

✔ To listen to native language patterns

✔ To "read" a book by independently turning the pages

✔ To engage in a conversation

MATERIALS:

❑ 1 or 2 cardboard books of nursery rhymes such as "Jack and Jill"

PREPARATION:

♡ Prop the books in a standing position and leave them slightly open. Displaying the book should help capture the child's attention.

NURTURING STRATEGIES:

1. When a child crawls near the books, move closer.
2. Observe the infant's interactions with the book.
3. Talk about the book the infant is looking at. Comment, for example:
   "That story is about Jack and Jill. Jack and Jill walk up a hill."
   "Victoria, that story is about pigs. The pigs go to the market."
4. Ask the infant:
   "May I read the book to you?"
   If the infant responds affirmatively, begin to read the book. If the infant responds negatively, allow the child to explore the book uninterrupted.
5. Using your voice as a tool to communicate enthusiasm may gain and sustain the infant's attention.
6. While reading the book, encourage the infant to turn the pages. Say, for example:
   "Victoria, turn the page. We've read these words."
   "What's going to happen next? Turn the page so we can read more."

7. Asking questions while reading may prompt the infant to babble. For example, while pointing to the picture, ask:
   "Victoria, who is that?"
   "What are they carrying?"
8. Providing positive reinforcement may result in the infant holding longer conversations. To illustrate, say:
   "That's right. Jill has a bucket."

☀ Highlighting Development

Repeated exposure to words and labeling people and objects will help foster language development in infants. The infants may accidentally begin stumbling on words. They may say "mama" for one of two reasons. Infants may be practicing the sounds by repeating the word over and over. On the other hand, some infants may have made the connection that words gain the attention of people who are important to them.

VARIATION:

♡ Introduce a book to a child if a quiet, calming activity is needed.

ADDITIONAL INFORMATION:

♡ Reading books of nursery rhymes is important because you have been reciting them for the past seven to eight months. The familiar words easily gain the infant's attention.

Goodnight

Child's Developmental Goals

✓ To listen to native language patterns
✓ To use books for relaxing

MATERIALS:

❑ *Goodnight Moon* board book by Margaret Wise Brown
❑ Rocking chair
❑ Security items needed for sleeping such as blanket, teddy bear, etc.

PREPARATION:

♡ Gather the security items and the book and position the rocking chair so that you are comfortable.

NURTURING STRATEGIES:

1. Pick up the infant and sit in the rocking chair.
2. Provide the infant with the security items. Talk in a quiet, soothing voice about nap time, while slowly rocking. Say, for example:
   "Jimmy, it is time to rest. You played hard today. You need to rest."
3. Once the child is relaxed, introduce the story by saying:
   "Jimmy, I picked out a story for us to read today. It is about going to sleep."
4. In a quiet, soothing voice, read the story.
5. Respond if the infant babbles, points, or otherwise attempts to communicate.
6. Avoid asking questions to engage the infant in babble or conversation because you are using the book as a calming tool.
7. If the infant is still awake, you may want to repeat the story.

Highlighting Development

Books can be used to excite children or calm them down. In fact, one book can be used for both purposes. Use your voice as a tool to communicate your intentions to the infant. Encourage the infant to assist in reading the book. Listen. Chances are the infant's babbling is following the intonation pattern of your reading.

VARIATION:

♡ Choose other books the infant enjoys. Refer to Appendix A for a list of books.

ADDITIONAL INFORMATION:

♡ Observe the children's reactions. They may have favorite books. Reading the same book over and over may be an enjoyable experience. Other hints for helping foster children's development of listening skills include:
   ✄ talking directly to the infant while making eye contact.
   ✄ using labels to help the infant associate names with objects and people in his environment.
   ✄ providing the infant an opportunity to touch objects while talking about them.
♡ When choosing books for children this age, look for those that are wrinkleproof, droolproof, and chewproof.

Look Who Walked In

Child's Developmental Goals

✓ To begin to associate words with people
✓ To reproduce the words "mama" and "dada"

MATERIALS:

None

PREPARATION:

♡ Prepare the child by talking about who will be coming.

NURTURING STRATEGIES:

1. Talk about who will be coming to visit the infant. Comment, for example:
   "Mama will be coming soon."
   "Dada is coming in the door."
2. Gain the infant's attention when the individual walks in the room by saying:
   "Kawanna, look who just walked in."
3. Reinforce the infant's babbles or vocalizations by stating:
   "You are excited to see Mama."
   "Yes, Dada is here to play with you."
4. Welcome the individual by singing the following song when the visitor enters:

   ♬ Hello, *Mama*,
   ♬ Hello, *Mama*,
   ♬ Hello, *Mama*,
   ♬ We're so glad you are here.

Highlighting Development

Attachment is the development of a bond between adults and children. The first and primary attachment is usually parents and children. Attachments are noticeable during separations and reunions. For example, when an important person is visible to the infant during a reunion, the infant may smile, babble, and, if able, move closer to that person.

VARIATION:

♡ When a person leaves, sing a good-bye song, such as:

   ♬ Good-bye *Terri*.
   ♬ Good-bye *Terri*.
   ♬ Good-bye *Terri*.
   ♬ We'll see you another day.

(Rhonda Whitman, Infant-Toddler Specialist University of Wisconsin–Stout)

ADDITIONAL INFORMATION:

♡ When interacting, provide the infant ample time to respond. Repeat people's names over so that the infant will understand that everybody has a name.

Cognitive Development

SEVEN to NINE MONTHS

Go Find It

Child's Developmental Goals

✓ To develop object permanence

✓ To engage in intentional behaviors

MATERIALS:

❑ Favorite infant toy

❑ Lightweight blanket

PREPARATIONS:

♡ Select an area that can be constantly supervised. Clear this area for the activity.

♡ Place the infant toy on the surface. Partially cover the toy with the blanket.

NURTURING STRATEGIES:

1. Encourage the infant to find a favorite toy. Say, for example:
   "Levi, go find Pooh bear. Look. Pooh is on the floor."
   "Crawl over by the blanket. Look."

2. Reinforce the infant's movement toward the blanket. For example, comments may include:
   "Levi, keep crawling."
   "You're almost there. Keep going."

3. Observe the infant's behaviors once he is near the blanket. If the infant moves the blanket, wait until the toy is uncovered. React with enthusiasm to the infant's discovery.

4. If the infant doesn't move the blanket, suggest that. Say, for example:
   "Levi, grab the blanket with your hands."
   "Move the blanket with your hands."

5. Reinforcing your words with actions may be necessary. For example, while gently placing the infant's hands on the blanket, say:
   "Levi, grab it." Pause. "Now pull the blanket."

6. Provide reinforcement for the infant's attempts and accomplishments. To illustrate, state:
   "Levi, that's it. Move the blanket."
   "Keep pulling! Almost there."

7. When the infant discovers the toy, react with enthusiasm. Say, for example:
   "You did it! You found Pooh."
   "Pooh was hiding from you!"

☀ Highlighting Development

Infants engage in goal-directed or intentional behaviors during this stage. In other words, when faced with a problem, they choose a particular way to solve the dilemma. For example, if a toy is hidden under a blanket, the infant may move the blanket aside to view the object.

VARIATIONS:

♡ Completely cover the toy with the blanket.

♡ Substitute blocks, small pots, or pans for the toy.

ADDITIONAL INFORMATION:

♡ This is a difficult activity. Providing plenty of reinforcement may keep the infant interested in the activity. Use your voice to convey your enthusiasm.

 Whenever pillows or blankets are used, constant supervision is necessary to prevent the possibility of suffocation.

Where Is It?

Child's Developmental Goals

✓ To develop an understanding of object permanence

✓ To engage in intentional behavior to solve a problem

MATERIALS:

❏ Piece of cardboard or shoe box lid

❏ Favorite infant toy

❏ Child-size table or low coffee table

PREPARATION:

♡ Clear an area for working at the table. Place the piece of cardboard and the infant toy in that work space.

NURTURING STRATEGIES:

1. Carry the infant to the table while talking about the activity. To illustrate, say:
    "Shalini, I have a special game just for you."
    "Let's play hide the giraffe."
2. Sit with pretzel legs at the table. Sit the infant in your lap. Move your body so that the infant is close to the table.
3. Gain the infant's attention by moving the toy and saying:
    "Shalini, here is your favorite toy. It is a giraffe."
4. Introduce the game by saying:
    "Shalini, I'm going to hide the giraffe. You find it."
5. Place the giraffe on the table and hold the cardboard with one hand in front of it. Encourage the infant to find the toy by commenting:
    "Find the giraffe. Look for it."
6. The infant may need suggestions on how to look for the toy. Comments to make include:
    "Shalini, move the cardboard."
    "Push the cardboard with your hand."

7. Reinforcing your words with actions may be necessary. If so, gently move the infant's hand while repeating:
    "Shalini, push the cardboard with your hand."
8. Provide positive reinforcement for all attempts and accomplishments. Enthusiastically state, for example:
    "Shalini, you did it! You found the giraffe."

☀ Highlighting Development

For infants a developmental task is the understanding that objects exist even when out of sight. In the beginning, infants can find objects that are partially hidden. During this stage, infants can find an object that is totally hidden from sight. However, the development of object permanence remains incomplete until the infant searches for the object when it is hidden in a second location.

Note the infant's behavior once objects are in hand. *Object hunger* is the term that describes the play behavior of infants at this stage of development. Infants orally examine objects by mouthing them, gaining physical knowledge about the objects.

VARIATION:

♡ Use a pillow or your body for hiding the toy. Encourage the infant to crawl or creep to find the toy.

ADDITIONAL INFORMATION:

♡ If the infants show more interest in pushing the cardboard than finding the object, this is acceptable. They will be practicing an important skill for locating desired objects.

♡ To gain understanding, infants perform similar experiences repeatedly.

Exploring Balls

COGNITIVE

Child's Developmental Goals:

✓ To engage in intentional behaviors

✓ To experience the principle of cause and effect

MATERIALS:

❑ 2 to 3 balls at least 6 inches in diameter

PREPARATION:

♡ Select an area that can be constantly supervised. Clear this area for the activity.

♡ Place the balls on the floor in this area.

NURTURING STRATEGIES:

1. Carry the infant to the selected area while talking about the activity. Say, for example:
   "Xui, I have some balls for you to play with."
   "Here are some balls. What can you do with them?"

2. Sit the infant on the floor while moving the balls within reach.

3. Observe the infant interacting with the balls.

4. Describe how the infant is exploring the balls. For example, comment:
   "Xui, you're touching the bumps with your fingertips."
   "That ball is smooth. You touched it with your tongue."

5. Reinforcing infant behaviors that accidentally occur may result in those behaviors being repeated. Comments include:
   "Xui, you pushed the ball. Do it again."
   "You're rolling the ball. Roll the ball to me."

6. Be prepared to retrieve the ball when it rolls out of the infant's reach or view.

Highlighting Development

With age, infants' ability to track moving objects improves. Their movements become more coordinated and smooth. Now infants can easily track the path of balls and other moving objects.

VARIATION:

♡ Use a toy with wheels instead of balls.

ADDITIONAL INFORMATION:

♡ Infants learn through repetition. Therefore, repeating this experience several times leads to expanded knowledge about oneself and objects in the environment.

🚫 Be sure to sanitize all toys that are touched by or placed in the infant's mouth.

7 to 9 months

What Is Inside the Box?

Child's Developmental Goals:

✓ To develop an understanding of object permanence

✓ To solve problems using intentional behaviors

MATERIALS:

❑ Shoe box with lid
❑ Favorite infant toy

PREPARATION:

♡ If desired, cover the shoe box and lid with colored, self-adhesive paper for aesthetic purposes.
♡ Place the toy in the box and replace the lid.

NURTURING STRATEGIES:

1. Gain the infant's attention by saying the child's name, shaking the box, and commenting:
   "Katisha, listen. What could be in the box?"
   "Look at my box. What do you hear?"

2. Encourage the infant to open the box and look inside. Say, for example:
   "Katisha, use your fingers. Pick up the lid."
   "Take off the lid. Look inside the box."

3. Using your voice as a tool to communicate excitement and pleasure may increase the infant's interest in the activity. To illustrate, when the infant removes the lid, say:
   "Katisha, you did it! You took off the lid."
   "Look at what's in the box? It's a ball."

4. If the infant seems interested, play the game again. To maintain interest, find a new toy to place in the box.

☀ Highlighting Development

Infants' attention spans are gradually improving. At the same time, they are differentiating themselves from the world. To illustrate, when discovering or finding a toy, infants may explore it with sucking actions. After this, they may alternate between sucking their thumb and sucking toys. In other words, at this stage of development, infants are learning to differentiate between their bodies and their environments.

VARIATIONS:

♡ Show the infant the toy and then place it inside the box. Encourage the infant to find the toy by removing the lid.
♡ Place the toy inside a gift bag and encourage the child to find the toy.

ADDITIONAL INFORMATION:

♡ Infants may spend more time playing with the box than trying to find the toy in the box. Removing and replacing objects are often enjoyable behaviors that infants attempt. These actions also promote the development of intentional behaviors.

Clapping the Lids

Child's Developmental Goals

✔ To repeat a behavior discovered by accident
✔ To practice clapping the hands together

MATERIALS:

❑ 2 lightweight metal saucepan lids

PREPARATION:

♡ Select and clear an area that can be constantly supervised. Place the lids in this area.

NURTURING STRATEGIES:

1. Gain the infant's attention by lightly clapping the lids together.
2. Suggest that the infant come over and play with the lids. To illustrate, say:
   "Ryan, crawl over here. You can bang the lids."
   "The lids are over here. Come play with them."
3. Observe the infant interacting with the lids.
4. If the infant is banging the lids together by using a clapping motion, provide positive reinforcement by saying:
   "Ryan, you're clapping the lids together. You're making music."
5. If the infant is making music in another way, provide time for exploration. Later, you might model how to use the lids.
6. Reinforcing your words with actions and assisting the infant may be necessary. If so, gently place each lid in the infant's hands while saying:
   "Ryan, clap your hands together."

7. Providing positive reinforcement may result in repetition of the behavior. Comments to make include:
   "Ryan, you did it. You're clapping the lids together."
   "Wow! Listen to the music you're making."

☀ Highlighting Development

Between seven and nine months of age, infants will continue repeating a behavior or reaction that was discovered by accident. To illustrate, after accidentally reaching for a bell hanging from an activity gym and obtaining a response, the infants will repeat the kicking motion, thereby learning a new behavior.

VARIATIONS:

♡ Provide a saucepan lid and a wooden spoon for making music.
♡ Repeat this activity in an outdoor area.

ADDITIONAL INFORMATION:

♡ This can be a very noisy activity. The infants will revel in their ability to make music. Therefore, this activity also fosters the development of self-esteem and self-efficacy.
♡ To enhance listening skills and promote auditory discrimination, provide toys that make sounds. Infants especially enjoy toys that make soft musical sounds or noise.

Coin Drop

Child's Developmental Goals

✓ To develop an understanding of object permanence

✓ To solve problems using intentional behaviors

MATERIALS:

❑ Oatmeal container with a plastic lid

❑ 4 to 5 juice can lids

PREPARATION:

♡ Carefully check the perimeter of the lids to make sure there are no sharp edges.

♡ Cut a slot in the top of a plastic oatmeal container lid so juice lids can easily be inserted.

♡ If desired, cover the oatmeal container with colored, self-adhesive paper for aesthetic purposes.

♡ Select an area that can be constantly supervised. Clear this area for the activity and place the oatmeal container and juice lids on the floor.

NURTURING STRATEGIES:

1. If the infant crawls near the materials for the activity, move closer.
2. Observe the infant's exploratory behavior with the materials.
3. If necessary, suggest that the infant put the juice lids into the container by saying:
   "Dakota, pick up the lid. Put it in the slot."
   "Put the lid inside the container."
4. Reinforcing your words with actions may be necessary. If so, point to the metal lids and touch the container while saying:
   "Dakota, put the lids through the slot."

5. Provide positive reinforcement for attempts or accomplishments. Comments to make include:
   "Good work. You put the lid inside the container."
   "Keep trying. You almost did it."
6. To foster the understanding of object permanence, ask the infant:
   "Dakota, where are the lids?"
7. Encourage the infant to turn the container upside down and shake the lids out. If necessary, model these actions.

☀ Highlighting Development

The principle of object permanence continues to develop during this period. Infants are learning that objects continue to exist even when out of sight. Playing games, such as hide-and-seek with toys, will help them practice the developing skills. Watch them. Independently, they will hide and find a wide variety of objects.

VARIATION:

♡ Use objects with different shapes such as plastic cookie cutters. Cut holes in the plastic lid to accommodate the shapes.

ADDITIONAL INFORMATION:

♡ Infants love hiding objects, especially when they are working on the concept of object permanence. Observe them. They will enjoy hiding and locating all types of objects.

Bring It to Me

COGNITIVE

Child's Developmental Goals

✓ To develop an understanding of object permanence

✓ To engage in intentional behaviors

✓ To obtain a desired object by moving one's body

MATERIALS:

☐ Infant toy that can be held while creeping such as large, plastic keys

PREPARATION:

♡ Place the toy 4 or 5 feet away from the infant. Be sure the toy is highly visible to the infant.

NURTURING STRATEGIES:

1. Gain the infant's attention by pointing to and verbally describing the toy. To illustrate, say:
   "Damon, the keys are on the carpet."
2. Encourage the infant to move closer to the keys. Suggest, for example:
   "Damon, pick up the keys."
   "Crawl over to the keys."
3. Observe the infant exploring the keys.
4. Describe how the infant is exploring the toys. Comments include:
   "Damon, you are touching the keys with your fingers."
   "You're chewing on the keys."

5. Encourage the infant to bring the toys to you. Comment, for example:
   "Damon, bring the toys to me."
   "Come to me. Bring the keys with you."
6. Reinforce the infant's attempts or accomplishments by saying:
   "Damon, you're doing it. Keep crawling. You are almost here."
   "Thank you. You brought me the keys."

☀ Highlighting Development

Infants need private time to play by themselves. They do not need to be constantly entertained. One of the most important skills is to self-entertain. Solitary playing will help lay a foundation for protecting them against boredom and loneliness later in life.

VARIATION:

♡ Ask the infant to pick up and hand you an object that you have dropped.

ADDITIONAL INFORMATION:

♡ Infants enjoy helping. Their new mobility and cognitive skills allow them to assist when given a reasonable, developmentally appropriate task.

♡ Cover the keys with a blanket to provide a challenge.

Social Development

SEVEN to NINE MONTHS

Rolling It Back

Child's Developmental Goals

✓ To interact with a familiar caregiver
✓ To develop a sense of trust

MATERIALS:

❑ Smooth, flat surface
❑ Clean ball, 6 to 12 inches in diameter

PREPARATION:

♡ Select a smooth, flat surface that will allow the ball to roll.

NURTURING STRATEGIES:

1. While carrying the infant to the designated area, talk about the activity. Comments include:
   "Ariel, let's play ball. We can roll it back and forth."
2. Sit the infant in the designated area. Position your body, allowing about 1 foot between you and the infant. Adjust yourself or the infant as needed.
3. Hand the ball to the infant.
4. Allow time for the infant to explore the ball. Comment on the infant's actions. For example, say:
   "Ariel, you are touching the ball with your fingers. The ball feels smooth."
   "Now you are hitting the ball."
5. Encourage the infant to roll the ball to you. Comments include:
   "Ariel, roll the ball to me. Push it."
   "Let's play a game. Roll the ball to me. Then, I'll roll it back."
6. Reinforce the infant's attempts and accomplishments. To illustrate, you might say:
   "Ariel, you made the ball roll."
   "You pushed the ball to me."
7. As long as the infant shows interest, continue the game by gently pushing the ball back and forth.

Highlighting Development

An infant's smile is reserved for special, familiar faces. This is the way the infant reaches out and rewards them. When the infant smiles, reinforce the importance of your relationship by talking and returning the smile.

VARIATIONS:

♡ As the infant progresses in the development of fine muscle skills, introduce balls that are smaller.
♡ Introduce this activity outdoors if conditions are appropriate.

ADDITIONAL INFORMATION:

♡ Infants learn to trust adults when their cues and signals are answered quickly and in a caring, responsive manner. Therefore, play this game only as long as the infant seems interested. Signs of interest to look for include smiling, maintaining eye contact, and babbling.

 Exercise caution with this activity, particularly if you introduce smaller balls. Never use a ball that could pose a choking hazard.

7 to 9 months

Peekaboo

Child's Developmental Goals

✓ To participate in a game

✓ To engage in social interaction with an adult

MATERIALS:

❑ Usual diapering supplies

PREPARATION:

♡ Prepare the diapering table to ensure the supplies are available.

NURTURING STRATEGIES:

1. While you are removing the child's clothing or the wet/dirty diaper, encourage the infant to hold the clean diaper. Say, for example:
   "Jesus, help me out. Hold your diaper."
2. Usually the infant will raise the diaper so that you can't see his face. When this happens, use your voice as a tool for communicating excitement by saying:
   "Where did Jesus go?"
3. When the infant lowers the diaper, say:
   "Jesus, peekaboo. I see you!"
4. Continue the interaction as long as the infant shows interest by laughing, smiling, or covering his face.
5. When interest in the game ceases, finish diapering the child.

☀ Highlighting Development

Because of their new abilities to anticipate events and engage in intentional behaviors, infants may now purposefully initiate social interactions. For example, watching a parent putting on a coat might result in crawling/creeping over and hugging the parent's legs in an attempt to maintain proximity.

VARIATION:

♡ Cover the infant's face with a favorite blanket and continue the game.

ADDITIONAL INFORMATION:

♡ Infants love to play peekaboo games. Responding to their bids to play the game will foster the development of self-efficacy skills. They will learn that they have some control over interactions with people in their environment.

7 to 9 months

Where Am I Hiding?

SOCIAL

Child's Developmental Goals

✓ To learn to cope with separation anxiety

✓ To act deliberately to maintain contact with an adult

MATERIALS:

None

PREPARATION:

♡ Observe the infant to determine the level of alertness.

NURTURING STRATEGIES:

1. Introduce the game to the infant. For example, tell the child:
   "Inez, I would like to play a game of hide- and-seek."

2. Ask the child to join in by saying:
   "Will you play with me?"

3. Explain the rules of the game by saying, for example:
   "Inez, I'll hide and you find me."

4. Using your knowledge of the child's development of object permanence, either hide completely or leave a body part easily visible.

5. When the infant finds you, react with enthusiasm. To illustrate, comment:
   "Inez, you found me. You knew exactly where to look."
   "You are good at this game."

6. Continue the game as long as the infant is interested.

 Highlighting Development

Hide-and-seek games help infants learn how the world works. They learn things exist even when out of sight. This knowledge will help them gradually develop the understanding that the world has some consistency and dependability.

VARIATION:

♡ When the game is understood, ask the child to hide an object.

ADDITIONAL INFORMATION:

♡ Mini-separations occur throughout the day. For example, you may need to diaper another child. If this occurs, continue talking to the infant to reduce separation anxiety.

♡ Continue playing hiding games and discussing the arrival and departure of people to help reinforce the principle of object permanence.

Measuring Water

Child's Developmental Goals

✓ To imitate an adult's action

✓ To engage in social interactions and play

MATERIALS:

❑ 1-cup measuring cup

❑ ½-cup measuring cup

❑ Large, nonbreakable mixing bowl

❑ Water

❑ Vinyl tablecloth

❑ Large bib

PREPARATION:

♡ Select an area that will not be damaged by water. Clear this area and spread out the vinyl tablecloth.

♡ Pour warm water in the bowl. Then place the bowl on the tablecloth.

♡ If the room is warm and free from draft, remove the infant's outer clothing. If these conditions are not present, roll the child's sleeves and put on a large bib.

NURTURING STRATEGIES:

1. Sit the infant close to the bowl on the tablecloth.
2. Encourage the infant to explore the materials. For example, ask:
   "Mike, what can you do with the cups?"
   "How does the water feel?"
3. Observe the infant's interactions with the materials.
4. Modeling new ways to hold the measuring cups may be necessary. For example, if the infant is holding the cup with the entire hand, demonstrate how to hold the handle using a pincer grasp.

5. If the infant continues to hold the cup in the same manner, verbally describe your actions by commenting, for example:
   "Mike, I'm holding the cup with my thumb and finger. Look at me. You try it."
   "Look at me. Try my way."
6. Providing positive reinforcement may encourage the infant to repeat the behavior. To illustrate, say:
   "Mike, you did it! We are holding the cups the same way."
   "Look at you. You're using your thumb."

☀ Highlighting Development

Given the development of motor skills, infants can now imitate the way adults use their hands. Showing them new skills may result in refining fine motor skills as well as adding new information to their self-identity.

VARIATIONS:

♡ Add large spoons to practice scooping the liquids. This may also help to foster the development of self-feeding skills.

♡ If outdoors, use a wading pool for water play to encourage the use of arm and leg movements.

ADDITIONAL INFORMATION:

♡ Infants enjoy the soothing sensation of water play.

 Infants can drown in as little as 1 inch of water; therefore, water play needs constant supervision. An adult should be within an arm's reach of the child.

I Am Here to Help

Child's Developmental Goals

✔ To use an adult as a secure base

✔ To continue developing a sense of trust

MATERIALS:

None

PREPARATION:

♡ Observe to see when adults or siblings are leaving.

NURTURING STRATEGIES:

1. Prepare the infant for the departure of a family member. Say, for example:
   "Grandpa will be leaving soon. Let's walk to the door and wave good-bye."
   "Aunt Lisa is going to school. Wave good-bye."

2. If the infant becomes upset at a family member's departure, pick up the child while talking in a soothing voice. Identifying the infant's emotions is important to the child understanding how she is feeling. For example, comment:
   "Xia, you are angry because Aunt Lisa left you. You wanted to go with her."
   "You are upset. You didn't want Grandpa to leave. You like spending time with Grandpa."

3. Let the infant know that you are there to help. Say, for example:
   "I'm here to help you."
   "It's okay to be sad. Let's rock for a while."

4. When the infant is ready to begin the day, encourage the child to explore the room. Suggest new things to look for around the room, by saying:
   "Xia, look at the new mirror."
   "I put out some new rattles."

5. Provide a secure base from which the infant can explore. Make comments such as:
   "I'm right here. I'll stay in the room. I'm not leaving."
   "I'll be right here if you need me."

6. As the infant explores the room, provide positive reinforcement. This may encourage the infant to explore for longer periods of time before "checking in" with you. To illustrate, say:
   "Xia, you are looking in the mirror. What can you see?"
   "You found the new rattle. What does it sound like?"

☀ Highlighting Development

During this period of development, infants begin to use familiar adults as secure bases. This means that the infants may leave the adult's side to explore their surroundings, but they frequently look back to check the adult's whereabouts. They also may move closer to the adult to make sure they are safe. Your reaction to their exploration or distance influences those factors. For example, displaying a fearful look may result in the infant moving closer to you.

VARIATION:

♡ Use family members' names when talking to the child. The infant needs to learn that everyone and everything has a name.

ADDITIONAL INFORMATION:

♡ During this time period, infants often experience separation anxiety. This occurs when a parent, guardian, or primary caregiver leaves their sight. Your role is to be supportive of these reactions while encouraging independence at the same time.

Stacking Cups

Child's Developmental Goals

✓ To interact socially with an adult

✓ To develop a sense of trust

MATERIALS:

❏ 1 set of stacking cups

PREPARATION:

♡ Select and clear an area that can be constantly supervised. Place the stacking cups in this area to motivate the infant.

NURTURING STRATEGIES:

1. As soon as an infant crawls near the area, move closer to provide assistance or support as needed.
2. Observe the infant's behaviors with the cups.
3. Describe what the infant is doing with the cups. Say, for example:
   "Jami, you are stacking the little cup on the big cup."
   "You are building a tower."
4. Ask questions or offer suggestions as necessary. Comments may include:
   "Where could you put this little cup?"
   "Stack this cup next."
   If necessary, point to the cup to continue maintaining his attention.
5. Talk about the child's reactions to the stacking cups. Say, for example:
   "Jami, you are smiling. You like stacking the cups."
   "How frustrating, the cups fell over. Try again."

6. Providing positive reinforcement may increase the infant's time at this activity. Say, for example:
   "Jami, keep trying. You've used all of the cups!"
   "You are working hard. You've stacked three cups!"

☀ Highlighting Development

Infants at this age prefer caregivers and parents to others. When familiar people are out of sight, they may cry and become irritable. This may cause you to feel guilty. By crying, the child is testing your behavior. Separation anxiety is more prevalent when infants are hungry, tired, or sick. Therefore, to reduce the effects of separation anxiety, it is important that the child is well rested and fed prior to your leaving.

VARIATION:

♡ For a new challenge, demonstrate how to nest the cups rather than stack them.

ADDITIONAL INFORMATION:

♡ Infants' newfound fine motor skills of pinching and releasing objects make this activity possible and successful. A supportive adult can assist the child in working through frustrations. To illustrate, when the stack tumbles over, you may have to assist the child.

7 to 9 months

Rolling Together

SOCIAL

Child's Developmental Goals

✓ To demonstrate interest in others

✓ To play a game

MATERIALS:

❑ 2 identical wheeled toys

PREPARATION:

♡ Select and clear an area that can be constantly supervised. Place the toys in this area.

NURTURING STRATEGIES:

1. Carry the infant to the designated area while talking about the planned activity. For example, say:
   "I have some toys for you to roll. You can push the toys back and forth."
2. Sit the infant close so that you are facing each other.
3. Hand the child a toy. Observe the infant exploring the toy.
4. Encourage the child to roll the toy to you. To illustrate, say:
   "Mai, roll your toy to me. Push it."
5. Providing positive reinforcement may encourage the infant to repeat the desired behavior. Comment, for example:
   "You did it Mai. Now I have both toys."
6. When the infant gazes at you or is engaged in the game, provide positive reinforcement. Doing this emphasizes the social interactions that are occurring. For example, state:
   "Mai, you are looking at me."
   "We are playing a game together."
   "We are pushing the toy back and forth. What a fun game."
7. Repeat the game as long as the infant seems interested.

☀ Highlighting Development

Infants are beginning to show interest in engaging in some basic interactions with others. For example, they look to others who are exhibiting signs of distress or happiness. Given their newly developed motor skills of crawling, they can now move toward others when interested.

VARIATION:

♡ Roll balls rather than wheeled toys.

ADDITIONAL INFORMATION:

♡ If the infant rolls the ball three or four times, this will be a highly successful activity.

♡ To encourage reaching, place push toys in front of the child. This will encourage full arm movements and forward motion.

 To promote safety, you should provide careful supervision. Otherwise, hair pulling, poking, and other behaviors can occur.

7 to 9 months

Emotional Development

SEVEN to NINE MONTHS

Making Music

Child's Developmental Goals

✓ To express the emotions of interest and enjoyment

✓ To express emotions in distinct, meaningful patterns

MATERIALS:

❑ 2 lightweight saucepans of varying sizes with lids

PREPARATION:

♡ Select and clear an area that can be constantly supervised. Place the pans and lids in this area.

NURTURING STRATEGIES:

1. When an infant crawls or creeps over to the pans, move closer to the child.
2. Observe the infant's interactions with the pans and lids.
3. If the child bangs them together to make a sound, provide positive reinforcement by saying:
   "Radi, you're making music!"
   "What a loud sound you make. Do it again!"
4. If the infant is exploring the toys in different ways, verbally encourage the child to bang the pans together. For example, comment:
   "Radi, hit the lid on the pan."
   "Bang the lid and pan together. You are making music that way."

5. Describe the child's reactions to the action. Comments might include:
   "Radi, you are laughing and smiling. You must really enjoy making music."
   "You are working hard to make music."
   "You are enjoying this activity."

☀ Highlighting Development

Infants may be afraid of loud noises such as those from thunder, the vacuum cleaner, car horns, firecrackers, etc. When this occurs, reach out to comfort them by cuddling and providing verbal assurance. Over time, the fears should gradually decrease with increased experiences.

VARIATION:

♡ Substitute nonbreakable, lightweight cereal or mixing bowls and wooden spoons for the saucepans and lids.

ADDITIONAL INFORMATION:

♡ Some infants may be frightened by loud noises. If so, provide tools that make quieter music. Gradually, you may build back up to the loud, noisy tools.

7 to 9 months

Jack-in-the-Box

Child's Developmental Goals

✓ To begin coping with the emotion of fear

✓ To express emotions in distinct, meaningful patterns

MATERIALS:

❑ Jack-in-the-box pop-up toy

PREPARATION:

♡ Select and clear an area that can be constantly supervised. Then place the jack-in-the-box toy in this area.

NURTURING STRATEGIES:

1. When the infant crawls over to the toy, move closer. Begin the activity by asking the infant questions about the toy. To illustrate, ask:
   "Kumiko, what is this?" Pause. *"It is a new toy."*
   "How does this toy work?"
   "What could you do with this handle?"
2. Observe the infant exploring the toy.
3. Provide suggestions on how to "open" the toy. Say, for example:
   "Kumiko, turn the handle."
   "Grab hold of the handle. Move your arm in a circle."
4. Reinforcing your words with actions may be necessary. If so, point to the handle while saying:
   "Grab and turn the handle."
   "Push the handle in a circle."
5. Describe how to make music using the toy. For example, comment:
   "Kumiko, look and listen. Turning the handle makes music."
   "Oh, listen to the music you're making."

6. Prepare the infant for Jack popping out of the toy by stating:
   "Kumiko, look. Something is going to happen."
   "Jack is going to pop out of the toy."
7. When Jack pops up, describe the infant's reactions. Say, for example:
   "That startled you. You moved your body backward."
8. Encourage the infant to find Jack again. To illustrate, say:
   "Where did Jack go? Let's find him again."
   "Turn the handle to find him."

☀ Highlighting Development

Infants express more fear from this time until about 18 months of age. This rise in fear is believed to be linked to the infant's abilities to distinguish between familiar and unfamiliar faces. This ability results in both stranger and separation anxiety.

VARIATIONS:

♡ Use a musical box or push-up toy.
♡ Introduce the child to other action toys. Infants may squeal in delight watching them move.

ADDITIONAL INFORMATION:

♡ Children may be fearful of this activity when it is first introduced. This is most likely related to their lack of understanding of object permanence. Repeated exposure to action toys such as the jack-in-the-box toy will usually result in enjoyment.
♡ For the first experience, turn and have Jack pop up from a distance to reduce the possibility of fear.

Popping It Up

Child's Developmental Goals

✓ To use the caregiver as a social reference point

✓ To express emotions in distinct, meaningful patterns

MATERIALS:

❑ 2 pop-up boxes

PREPARATION:

♡ Select and clear an area that can be constantly supervised. Place the toys on a child-size shelf or the floor.

NURTURING STRATEGIES:

1. When an infant crawls or creeps into the area, position yourself so you are closer to the child.
2. Describe the toy for the infant. Say, for example:
   "Graham, if you push this button, something will happen."
   "If you turn this knob, something will pop up."
3. Observe the infant interacting with the toy.
4. Reinforcing your words with actions may be necessary. To illustrate, model pushing the button, while saying:
   "When I push the button, something pops up."
5. Reacting with excitement for the infant models how to respond when unexpected things happen. When the infant looks at you, you are being used as a social reference point.
6. Encourage the infant to push the button by saying:
   "Graham, you do it now. Push the button with your hand."
   "You try it. Show me where the Mickey Mouse is hiding."

7. Providing positive reinforcement may result in the infant repeating the behavior independently. Comments might include:
   "You found where it was hiding."
   "You did it! You found the Mickey Mouse."
8. Describing the infant's reactions to this behavior may help the child to better understand emotions. To illustrate, say:
   "Graham, you are excited because you found the Mickey Mouse."
   "You are laughing and smiling. You must like this toy."

☀ Highlighting Development

During this stage, infants begin to anticipate routine activities. To illustrate, when a bottle is filled by the caregiver, the infant may crawl over, sit up, and reach for the bottle. When a doorbell rings, the infant may crawl or creep to the door. Likewise, when playing with action toys, the infant might anticipate the objects popping up.

VARIATION:

♡ Use other pop-up or action toys to stimulate the infant's emotional expressions.

ADDITIONAL INFORMATION:

♡ During this time period, infants will be dependent on you for information on how to react to new or unusual experiences or objects. In other words, the infants use others as social reference points. Therefore, modeling excitement or interest may encourage infants to actively explore their environment and reduce their fears of new experiences.

EMOTIONAL

A Stranger among Us

Child's Developmental Goals

✓ To begin coping with stranger anxiety

✓ To express the emotion of fear

MATERIALS:

None

PREPARATION:

♡ Tell the child that a visitor will be arriving.

NURTURING STRATEGIES:

1. When a stranger enters the room, prepare yourself for the infant's reaction. The infant might cry or move closer to you.
2. Position yourself so you can make eye contact with the infant. Then introduce the infant to the stranger. This will let the infant know that you know who this person is. Say, for example:
   "Elma, this is my friend Houa. He is coming to pick up Vang."
   "This is my friend Tammy. She came to help make snack."
3. Comfort the child by remaining close and talking in a soothing voice. Make comments such as:
   "It's okay to be afraid, Elma."
   "New faces can be scary."
4. Be sure to remind the infant that she is safe. State, for example:
   "I'm here to help. Tammy is my friend."
   "I will hold you while she is here."

☼ Highlighting Development

Prior to this stage of development, infants emoted by using their entire body. Now they are beginning to express emotions in distinct, coherent patterns. They can combine facial expression, gaze, voice, and posture to communicate one message. To illustrate, when a stranger enters a child's visual path, she may respond by crying and looking at and moving closer to you.

VARIATIONS:

♡ Introduce the child to all the new faces she comes in contact with.

♡ Alter your language to reflect the relationship between the visitor and the child: mother, father, aunt, uncle, etc.

ADDITIONAL INFORMATION:

♡ Strangers such as neighbors, friends, mail carriers, and delivery people come and go frequently. Your job is to help infants cope with seeing new faces. Warm, caring interactions will help them to know they are safe.

I Found Something New

EMOTIONAL

Child's Developmental Goals

✓ To express the emotion of interest
✓ To self-regulate through mobility

MATERIALS:

❑ Favorite infant toy

PREPARATION:

♡ Select an area that can be constantly supervised. Clear this area and place the toy there.

NURTURING STRATEGIES:

1. Observe the infant's behaviors in the room.
2. When the infant needs something new to play with, encourage the child to find a favorite toy. Say, for example:
   "Where is the drum? Keep looking."
   "Look around. Find the drum, Brian. Move closer so you can play with it."
3. Reinforce the infant's attempts and accomplishments by saying:
   "Brian, you found the drum."
   "You found something new to play with by crawling."
4. The goal is to encourage the infant to find things of interest independently. Reach this long-term goal by saying things such as:
   "You were bored. You found something new and interesting to play with."
   "When you get tired of one toy, look for another."

☀ Highlighting Development

Because most infants can crawl now, they are able to self-regulate. They can leave a situation that is overwhelming, or they can join one that is inviting.

VARIATIONS:

♡ To maintain interest, rotate the infant's toys.
♡ Instead of commercial toys, provide the child with common household items. Examples include cups, saucers, wooden spoons, pots, and pans.

ADDITIONAL INFORMATION:

♡ Once they are mobile, infants often move from one activity to another. The goal is to have toys available that will sustain their interest.
♡ The beginnings of behavior and impulse control typically occur between eight or nine months of age. The infant will respond to caregivers who encourage them to look with their eyes.

7 to 9 months

A New Friend

Child's Developmental Goals

✓ To begin coping with stranger anxiety

✓ To use an adult as a social reference point

MATERIALS:

❑ Infant stroller

PREPARATION:

♡ Tell the infant that a stroller ride is planned.

♡ Secure the infant in the stroller using the safety restraints.

NURTURING STRATEGIES:

1. Talk to the infant about where you are going and why. Say, for example:

   "We are taking a stroller ride. We are going to Mrs. Nicholson's store. She sells us bread. She is my friend. I want you to meet her."

2. Upon arrival at the bakery, greet your friend. Model excitement or enjoyment by smiling, shaking hands, and maintaining eye contact. When watching you interact, the child is using you as a social reference.

3. Talk with Mrs. Nicholson for two or three minutes to allow the infant time to get comfortable with the stranger.

4. Tell her that you would like to introduce someone. Say, for example:

   "Mrs. Nicholson, this is Jasmine. She likes to take stroller rides."

5. Observe the infant's reactions to the stranger. Provide support as necessary. To illustrate, state:

   "It's okay to be afraid. I'm here to help. Mrs. Nicholson is my friend."

6. Thank Mrs. Nicholson for her time and say to the infant:

   "Let's continue riding in the stroller. Where should we go next?"

☀ Highlighting Development

Strangers and parents often do not understand why infants become upset at the presence of new people. You need to help them understand this is a normal stage that infants go through. Given time and repeated experiences, the infants will gradually reduce their fear of the unknown.

VARIATION:

♡ Take trips to the post office, store, restaurant, shopping malls, etc.

ADDITIONAL INFORMATION:

♡ Infants need to learn skills for coping with strangers. Begin by introducing new people in safe and supportive environments.

Jazzing It Up!

Child's Developmental Goals

✓ To experience different types of music
✓ To practice self-soothing techniques

MATERIALS:

❑ Tape or compact disc player
❑ Tape or compact disc of music such as *Lullabies Go Jazz* by Jon Crosse

PREPARATION:

♡ Select an outlet for plugging in the tape or compact disc player. Make sure a high cabinet or shelf is nearby to place the player safely out of the infant's reach.

♡ Put the tape or compact disc in the player and plug it in.

NURTURING STRATEGIES:

1. Dim the lights and turn on the tape player.
2. Lay the infant faceup in the crib.
3. Gently rub the infant's belly.
4. Using a gentle, soothing voice, talk about the music. Say, for example:
   "Listen to the music. The saxophone is soothing."
   "What a pretty lullaby. Relax. Listen to the music."
5. Allow the infant to use the music to relax and fall asleep. Therefore, you should leave before the infant falls asleep.

☀ Highlighting Development

During this time, infants may begin to express anger. This feeling often arises when infants are trying to accomplish a goal and are ineffective. Given their cognitive abilities to engage in intentional behaviors, they may also express anger when their goals are blocked. Adults often block infants' goals when they are unresponsive to their cues. An example would include making them take a nap when their bodies are rested.

VARIATIONS:

♡ Encourage the infant to imitate your humming to the music.

♡ Introduce different types of music such as classical music or nature tapes.

ADDITIONAL INFORMATION:

♡ This tape is useful when infants need quiet, relaxing activities. Refer to the Introduction (see pp. 10–11) for additional suggestions for soothing a crying infant.

Physical Development

TEN to TWELVE MONTHS

Filling and Dumping

PHYSICAL

Child's Developmental Goals

✓ To practice releasing objects by opening the fingers

✓ To deliberately place an object in a container

MATERIALS:

☐ Foam blocks

☐ Large plastic container

PREPARATION:

♡ Select and clear an area that can be constantly supervised.

♡ Place the plastic container in the middle of the cleared area. Scatter the foam blocks on the floor around the container.

NURTURING STRATEGIES:

1. When the infant moves closer to the area, position yourself so you are able to observe the infant's behavior with the materials.

2. If the infant explores the blocks as opposed to filling the container, watch him. Later, suggest filling the container by saying:
   "Lucien, put the blocks in this container."

3. Reinforcing your words with actions may be necessary. If so, model picking up the blocks and releasing them into the container while saying:
   "Let's fill up the container with the blocks."

4. Provide positive reinforcement for attempts or accomplishments. Comments might include:
   "Lucien, you are working hard. The container is almost full."
   "You are placing the blocks in the container."
   "Look at you! You've picked up all the blocks."

5. If the infant seems interested, dump out the container and begin the game again.

☀ Highlighting Development

At about 10 months of age, infants learn to voluntarily release objects held in their hands. Observe them. They spend a significant amount of time concentrating on picking up and releasing objects.

VARIATIONS:

♡ Enlist the infant's help to fill containers during cleanup time.

♡ Introduce variety by providing the child rubber or plastic toys to put in the container.

ADDITIONAL INFORMATION:

♡ Infants might need help releasing the blocks from their hand. You can assist in one of two ways. First, you can place your hand under the object in the infant's hand. Second, you can suggest that the infant place the object in the bottom of the container. A firm surface usually stimulates infants to open their hands.

♡ Once the child is interested, you can leave him with the blocks and container to repeat and practice independently.

♡ With practice, the child's movements will become more coordinated and efficient.

♡ Blocks are response toys that teach spatial relationships and cause and effect.

10 to 12 months

Letting Go

Child's Developmental Goals

✓ To develop the voluntary release of hand muscles

✓ To refine the development of fine motor skills

MATERIALS:

❑ Complicated infant toy.

PREPARATION:

♡ Observe the child for times of alertness. Make sure the toy you select has been cleaned and sanitized.

NURTURING STRATEGIES:

1. When the infant needs a toy to explore, provide the toy you selected while saying:
   "Vivaca, here is a new toy for you."
   "Look at this new toy. Feel it with your fingers."

2. Observe the infant exploring the toy. Note the infant's exploration style such as mouthing and touching it with a finger.

3. Provide language stimulation by describing what the infant is doing. Say, for example:
   "You are touching the toy with your pointer finger."
   "You are holding the toy in your left hand."
   "You are touching your tongue to the small circle."

4. Practice voluntary release by asking the infant to hand you the toy while extending your hand.

5. It may be necessary to assist the infant in releasing the toy. If so, place your hand under the object and apply gentle pressure to create a firm surface.

6. Reinforcing the infant's attempts and accomplishments may encourage the behaviors to be repeated. To illustrate, say:
   "Vivaca, you did it! You gave me the toy."
   "You are working hard. Keep trying."

7. If the infant continues to appear interested, hand the toy to the child, thereby repeating the interaction.

☀ Highlighting Development

At this developmental stage, infants are learning to voluntarily release their grasp. When holding a foam block in their hand, for example, they can open their hand, causing the block to be released.

VARIATION:

♡ Introduce a favorite toy from the past.

ADDITIONAL INFORMATION:

♡ Continue to connect behaviors with actions by describing what the child is doing.

♡ When choosing toys for infants, construction is an important consideration. Choose toys that are durable and can withstand enthusiastic handling (Abrams & Kaufman 1990).

10 to 12 months

Dropping Objects

10 to 12 months

Child's Developmental Goals

✓ To practice releasing objects by opening the fingers

✓ To practice problem solving by pulling on a string to get a desired object

MATERIALS:

☐ 3 infant toys

☐ 3 three-foot pieces of wool yarn

PREPARATION:

♡ Select a piece of yarn and tie it to one end of the infant toy. Attach by tying the free end of the yarn to an arm of the high chair. Repeat this procedure with the other pieces of yarn and toys.

♡ Place the infant in the high chair, securing the child with the safety strap. Position and lock the tray in place.

NURTURING STRATEGIES:

1. While placing each toy on the tray, talk about it. Say, for example:
   "Hugh, here is a stuffed dinosaur."
   "You like this toy. It is a cow. Cows say moo."

2. Explain to the child what to do if the toy is dropped over the edge. Comments may include:
   "Hugh, look at the toys. They are on strings. Pull the string."
   "If it falls, pull on this string."

3. Reinforcing your words with actions may be necessary. If so, while touching the toy, say:
   "Watch me pull on the string."

4. Watch the infant exploring and dropping the objects.

5. Respond to the infant's vocalizations. If the infant is interested or excited, comment:
   "Hugh, you found the cow!"
   "You like this game!"
   If the infant becomes frustrated, remind the child what to do using a warm and supportive voice. For example, say:
   "Pull the string."
   "You can do it. Find the cow."

☀ Highlighting Development

Infants are perfecting their skills when they drop objects. These actions teach them cause and effect. Each time an item hits the surface, children see an immediate response as a result of their actions. If the adult immediately picks up the object, the action is likely to be repeated becoming a game. Often this game will be accompanied by expressions of positive emotions such as laughing or squealing with delight.

VARIATION:

♡ Secure a favorite toy to the crib with short pieces of wool yarn.

ADDITIONAL INFORMATION:

♡ Infants naturally drop things from the high chair. Therefore, this activity builds upon this interest.

♡ Whenever possible, admire the child's accomplishments.

 Using wool yarn reduces safety concerns because it will break before it reaches a strangling point.

Basket Throw

Child's Developmental Goals

✓ To practice throwing an object
✓ To refine walking skills

MATERIALS:

❑ Laundry basket with sturdy sides
❑ 6 to 8 tennis or lightweight balls

PREPARATION:

♡ Clear an area for the basket. If indoors, place the basket near a wall for a backboard. If outdoors, place it along a fence or building.
♡ Place the tennis balls on the ground around the basket.

NURTURING STRATEGIES:

1. When the infant walks or crawls over to the area, move closer.
2. Introduce the activity by saying:
   "Dera, this is a game. Throw the balls in the basket. How many balls can you put in the basket?"
3. Demonstrate the activity and then encourage the child to throw the ball in the basket.
4. Count the number of balls that land in the basket.
5. Provide positive reinforcement for attempts or accomplishments. Comments to say include:
   "Dera, you threw the ball into the basket."
   "One. Two. Three. Three balls are in the basket."
   "You've thrown all the balls in the basket."
   "You're helping to pick up the balls."

 Highlighting Development

When first learning to throw, children are uncoordinated. They often drop the ball behind them or at arm's length in front of them because they are experimenting with the timing of when to release their grip. This is normal behavior and, with practice, they will learn when to release.

VARIATION:

♡ Introduce bigger balls such as soccer balls or basketballs to promote the development of large muscle skills.

ADDITIONAL INFORMATION:

♡ Young children find throwing exciting. Watch them. Their pleasure is reflected in their facial expressions. Moreover, they are devoted to the activity.

10 to 12 months

Scribble Table

Child's Developmental Goals

✓ To refine fine motor skills

✓ To practice standing at a table using one hand for support

MATERIALS:

❑ Piece of newsprint or light-colored butcher paper large enough to cover the entire table

❑ Masking tape

❑ Red, green, blue, and orange chunky crayons

❑ Plastic container

❑ Child-size table or coffee table

PREPARATION:

♡ Cover the table with the paper and secure with masking tape.

♡ Place the crayons in the container and on the table approximately 5 to 6 inches from the edge, allowing the child to conveniently reach them.

NURTURING STRATEGIES:

1. When a child crawls or toddles over to the table, introduce the activity by saying:
   "Mateo, watch me. Use the crayons. Mark on the paper."
2. Encourage the infant to choose a crayon from the container. To illustrate, say:
   "Choose a crayon."
   If necessary, move the container closer.
3. Label the crayon chosen by the infant and say:
   "Mateo, you chose a blue crayon."
4. Observe the infant working. Provide the child time to think about the artwork. Then describe the motions or markings by saying:
   "You are using your arm to draw a circle."
   "You are making long lines. The lines go from side to side."
5. Providing positive reinforcement may extend the infant's participation in the activity. Comments include:
   "Mateo, you are working hard."
   "You've used three different colors: red, blue, and orange."

6. Before interest is lost in the activity, print the infant's name near the markings. Model proper writing skills by capitalizing the first letter of the name and using lowercase letters for the rest. Likewise, because in our culture we write from left to right, place the child's name in the upper left-hand corner. In addition, say each letter as you write it.
7. To boost the child's self-esteem, point to the name and markings, while smiling and saying, for example:
   "Mateo, you made all of these marks! You should be proud."

☀ Highlighting Development

During this stage, infants are perfecting their newly acquired fine muscle skills. The ability to mark with crayon is possible once the pincer grasp is developed. As with other activities, they will enjoy the cause and effect of scribbling. The infants can see that marks are created by using their hands.

VARIATIONS:

♡ After covering the table with newspaper, tape down individual pieces of paper for the child to decorate.

♡ Introduce this activity with the child sitting in the high chair.

ADDITIONAL INFORMATION:

♡ The choice of crayons and paper is important when working with infants. Using dark crayons on light paper increases the chance of infants' light marks being visible. In addition, using fat or chunky crayons is necessary because of the infants' fine motor skills.

♡ Write the date the child completed the artwork on it. By collecting samples of work over time, you will be able to observe the infant's developmental accomplishments.

♡ To prevent scribbling on walls, floors, or furniture, activities with crayons should always be carefully supervised.

Cruising Time

Child's Developmental Goals

✓ To practice pulling self to a standing position by using a table

✓ To practice "cruising" along the edge of the table

MATERIALS:

❑ Sturdy child-size table or coffee table

PREPARATION:

♡ Clear the table and the area around the table.

NURTURING STRATEGIES:

1. When the infant is attempting to pull up on an unsturdy item, redirect the child by carrying her to the table and saying:
   "Lian, the table is safe. Pull yourself up using the table."
2. Stay close while the child is working because the child may lose her balance and fall backward.
3. Observe the infant's behavior. If necessary, provide a few verbal suggestions to assist the child. Be sure to not overwhelm the infant with suggestions. Infants learn best through trial and error and practice. For example, suggest:
   "Lian, use both hands."
   "Push up with your legs."
4. Provide positive reinforcement for attempts and accomplishments. Comments include:
   "Look at you! You're standing."
   "You're using the table to walk."
   "You can walk fast using the table."
   "You're working hard."
5. When you think the infant is becoming tired or wants to change the activity, help the child return to a sitting position.

6. Close the activity by saying things such as:
   "Lian, you worked hard today pulling up."
   "You are really practicing walking."
7. If needed, help the infant transition to another activity. For example, say:
   "You are tired after that activity. Do you want to look at some books?"

☼ Highlighting Development

A word of caution: Avoid hurrying infants toward independent standing or walking. Positioning an infant into a standing position seldom results in the learned behavior. Infants will pull themselves into a standing position when developmentally ready and given the opportunity. Providing sturdy furniture such as a coffee table or couch will support this development (Leach, 1992).

VARIATION:

♡ Help the infant pull up and cruise along a sturdy structure outdoors.

ADDITIONAL INFORMATION:

♡ This is a very strenuous physical activity for infants. Therefore, they may be extra tired or hungry after participating in this activity.

♡ Once infants pull themselves to a standing position, they are unable to sit back down because they need their hands for support. You will often need to help them move back into a sitting position.

♡ Infants should have access to furniture that will assist them in pulling up to a standing position.

10 to 12 months

Walking during the Snack-Time Routine

PHYSICAL

10 to 12 months

Child's Developmental Goals

✓ To walk with assistance

✓ To develop balance in an effort to stand or walk unassisted

MATERIALS:

None

PREPARATION:

♡ Warn the infant that snack time will be in a few minutes and it will be necessary to stop playing and wash hands.

NURTURING STRATEGIES:

1. Assist the infant in preparing for snack by saying: *"Kwame, it is snack time. You will need to wash your hands."*

2. Encourage the infant to walk with you to the bathroom or sink by extending your hands and saying:
   "Give me your hands. Let's walk together."
   "We will walk to the sink together, Kwame."

3. Using both hands, gently pull the infant to a standing position and begin walking to the sink.

4. Providing positive reinforcement may make the infant feel good about the newly acquired skills and, thereby, increase self-esteem. To illustrate, say:
   "What a good walker you are."
   "You are working hard."
   "Kwame, you are strong."

5. Wash and dry the infant's hands.

6. Repeat step 4 while walking to the snack area.

☀ Highlighting Development

Motor skills work as a system. More advanced skills are developed when separate systems blend together and cooperate with others. Thus, prior to walking, a child needs to sit and stand.

After crawling, most infants begin walking by supporting themselves on furniture. By 11 months, they can walk when their hand is held and they are led. Most infants can walk on their own by their first birthday (Berk, 1997).

VARIATION:

♡ Help the infant walk during other transitions, such as nap time, outdoor play, etc.

ADDITIONAL INFORMATION:

♡ Infants should be encouraged, but not forced, to practice walking during different routines throughout the day. Crawling or creeping should be encouraged while playing; these types of locomotion are necessary for brain development because they exercise both sides of the body and brain simultaneously.

♡ Children learn lessons about balance and gravity by moving their bodies through space.

 To prevent accidents, paths should be kept clear so that children do not bump into furniture.

Language and Communication Development

TEN to TWELVE MONTHS

Dressing to Go Outside

Child's Developmental Goals

✓ To increase receptive language skills
✓ To demonstrate an understanding of words

MATERIALS:

None

PREPARATION:

♡ Make sure the child has the appropriate clothing for outdoor play.

NURTURING STRATEGIES:

1. Warn the child that a change in activities is coming by saying, for example:
   "Ashley, in a few minutes we are going to clean up. Then we will get ready to go outside."

2. After a few minutes, begin singing a cleanup song, such as:

   ♫ Clean up, clean up.
   ♫ Everybody everywhere
   ♫ Clean up, clean up.
   ♫ Everybody do your share.

   Sing this as long as it takes to pick up all of the toys.

3. After the toys are picked up, say, for example:
   "Let's get ready to go outside. What do we need? It is windy today. Get your hat and jacket."

4. Encourage the child to get the necessary items by saying:
   "Ashley, let's go get your hat."
   "Come over here. You need to get your coat."

5. Provide positive reinforcement when the child retrieves an item of clothing. These actions will show the infant's new level of independence. Reinforce their actions by saying:
   "Here is your hat. We found it."

6. Assist the child in putting on the clothes and going outside.

Highlighting Development

An infant begins to point at about 11 months of age. Pointing is used as a communication tool to direct your attention to another object or person at a distance. Observe the infant during this process. Typically, she will look at you while pointing and immediately after. The infant is interested in knowing whether she has redirected your attention. Listen. At this stage, the infant makes prelinguistic speech, which is referred to as echolalia. This begins occurring at about 9 to 10 months of age. The infant will consciously imitate the sounds of others. However, this occurs without understanding (Bentzen, 2001).

Studies show that the earlier an infant begins to point, the more words she knows by two years of age (Butterworth, 1997).

VARIATION:

♡ This activity can be repeated when undressing after coming in from playing outdoors.

ADDITIONAL INFORMATION:

♡ Children need to have warnings that transitions are coming. These warnings will help them finish the activity and start a new one.

♡ Encourage the infants to participate in as much of the dressing and undressing as possible. This promotes feelings of independence.

That's What I Want

Child's Developmental Goals

✓ To use gesturing skills to achieve a desired outcome

✓ To add to the repertoire of receptive language skills

MATERIALS:

None

PREPARATION:

♡ Carefully observe the infant.

NURTURING STRATEGIES:

1. When a child points to an object or otherwise gestures a need, respond by elaborating or explaining his need. To illustrate, say:
   "You are pointing at the box of crackers. Cody, are you hungry? Do you want a cracker?"
2. Reinforce the infant's behaviors by saying:
   "This is a cracker. You pointed to the box of crackers."
3. Assist the infant in obtaining the desired outcome by, in this example, handing the infant the cracker.
4. Observe the infant. If still hungry, the child may gesture for a second cracker. If this happens, ask:
   "Cody, do you want another cracker?"

☀ Highlighting Development

Infants show their knowledge of language through the use of preverbal gestures. To illustrate, they may point to an item of interest. These gestures are typically accompanied by babbling. Labeling these gestures assists in the development of receptive and expressive language skills.

VARIATION:

♡ Reinforce your words with gestures when giving instructions to an infant. For example, while saying, "Put the truck on the shelf," place your hand on the shelf.

ADDITIONAL INFORMATION:

♡ Infants will quickly learn that words are more effective than gestures. Therefore, this activity also promotes the development of expressive language skills.

♡ During this stage infants begin deliberately using nonverbal actions to convey meanings. To illustrate, they will shake or turn their head away to indicate no. They may wave bye-bye. Hand gestures are also used with an accompanying "ah ah ah." The "ah ah ah" means they want something such as a toy or cracker. Whenever this occurs, the caregiver should respond with words.

10 to 12 months

More, More, More

10 to 12 months

Child's Developmental Goals

✓ To express desires verbally

✓ To communicate through gestures

MATERIALS:

❏ Nutritious snack on a small plate

❏ Pitcher of juice and cup with lid

PREPARATION:

♡ Prepare the snack and position the high chair next to a table. Sanitize the high chair and wash the child's hands.

NURTURING STRATEGIES:

1. Place the child in a high chair using the safety restraint.
2. Place a small, nonbreakable plastic plate with the snack and cup on the tray of the high chair.
3. Observe the child eating snack.
4. If the child gestures or vocalizes for more food, respond by saying:
    "Lara, what do you want?"
5. Encourage the child to verbally respond. Make comments such as:
    "Tell me what you want."
6. If the infant gestures, verbally label the actions. Comments include:
    "Lara, you are pointing at the pitcher. Do you want more juice?"
    "You are pointing at the crackers. Do you want more crackers?"

7. If necessary, provide the words for the infant. To illustrate, say:
    "More. More juice. You want more juice."
    "More. Crackers. You want more crackers."
8. Of course, provide the infant with the desired item.

☀ Highlighting Development

Infants' first words appear, on average, at about 12 months. These words tend to refer to important people (*mama, grandpa*), actions (*bye-bye, no*), or moving objects (*ball, car*).

VARIATION:

♡ Repeat this activity during breakfast, lunch, or dinner.

ADDITIONAL INFORMATION:

♡ Encourage the child's communication efforts as well as accomplishments by sharing your enthusiasm through your voice and facial expressions.

 Observe to see that the child does not choke.

Animal Sounds

Child's Developmental Goals

✓ To continue developing receptive language skills

✓ To practice responding to questions

MATERIALS:

❑ Cardboard book with familiar animals such as dogs, cats, or farm animals

PREPARATION:

♡ Display the book in an area of the room where the child can easily access it. This allows it to be selected by the infant.

NURTURING STRATEGIES:

1. When the book is chosen, position yourself so you can observe the child exploring the book.
2. Offer to read the book to the infant by saying:
   "Oliver, would you like me to read the book to you?"
3. If the infant responds "no" by shaking the head or saying "no," offer to be available to read. For example, state:
   "I'll be over here if you change your mind."
4. The infant may respond by saying "yes," nodding his head, or handing you the book. When this occurs, sit down beside the infant making sure you can view any other children you are caring for.
5. Begin reading the book.
6. While reading, ask questions about the pictures. For example, ask:
   "Oliver, what sound does a cow make?"
   "What animal is this?"
7. Providing positive reinforcement will assist the infant in developing expressive language skills. For example, comment:
   "That's right! A cow says moo."
   "Yes. That is a duck."
8. Read the book again if the infant seems interested.

Highlighting Development

Asking questions helps to direct the child's attention. Questioning also stimulates the development of language skills. During this time, infants are more likely to respond with gesturing. During the second year of life, a child begins to respond with recognizable words.

VARIATION:

♡ While singing the song "Old MacDonald," encourage infants to make the animal sounds.

ADDITIONAL INFORMATION:

♡ Stimulate the infant's language development by reading to the infant throughout the day. If a book is unavailable, recite a favorite story or nursery rhyme. The value of these activities cannot be overlooked. They expose the infant to his native language and promote the development of both receptive and expressive language skills.

♡ Show the child how to turn the pages of the book. If the child wants to assist, provide encouragement.

♡ The availability of books is important. The child may want to look at them independently. They may view them by holding the book upside down or turning several pages at a time. This is typical behavior.

10 to 12 months

"This Is the Way"

Child's Developmental Goals

✓ To continue developing receptive language skills

✓ To imitate another person's behavior/actions

MATERIALS:

❑ A carpet piece, large towel, blanket, or rug

❑ Picture of items in song, including a toothbrush, hairbrush, and spoon

PREPARATION:

♡ Collect all the materials and place them in an area where they are easily accessible.

NURTURING STRATEGIES:

1. Prepare the room. Then gain the child's attention by sitting on the floor and laying out the objects.

2. Invite the child to sing with you.

3. Introduce the song by saying:
   "Murphy, I have a song for us to sing today."

4. While singing the song, hold up the prop that accompanies the verse.

   ♫ This is the way we brush our teeth,
   ♫ brush our teeth, brush our teeth.
   ♫ This is the way we brush our teeth
   ♫ so early in the morning.

   Additional verses include actions such as:
   Brush our hair (or comb our hair)
   Put on clothes
   Eat our breakfast
   Wash our hands
   Drive to school
   Exercise

5. Encourage the infant to join in the activity by making comments such as:
   "Show me how you brush your teeth."

6. If the child seems interested, introduce the song again later in the day.

☀ Highlighting Development

A child's first word appears usually at about 12 months of age. These words typically are related to actions, people, or objects. Therefore, action songs help the child develop receptive and expressive language skills.

VARIATION:

♡ Continue adding verses such as take a nap, eat our cereal, etc.

ADDITIONAL INFORMATION:

♡ Infants have short attention spans. Consequently, they are able to sit only for short periods of time, usually only a few minutes. Therefore, keep the activities short. If the child likes the activity, repeat it again at a later time.

♡ Songs such as this, if sung in the order of your daily routines, help children develop a sense of time. They learn that one action precedes another.

10 to 12 months

Animal Puppets

Child's Developmental Goals

✓ To continue developing expressive language skills

✓ To continue increasing receptive language skills

MATERIALS:

❑ 2 animal puppets

❑ 2 empty and sanitized liquid soap containers close to the size of the puppets

PREPARATION:

♡ Place the puppets over the top of the sanitized liquid soap containers. Then display the puppets in an area where they will attract the child's attention.

NURTURING STRATEGIES:

1. When you see a child select a puppet from the shelf, move closer and invite yourself to play by saying:
   "Ahmed, can I play puppets with you?"

2. If the child indicates "no" either verbally or with his body language, then say:
   "I'll just watch you play."

3. If the child uses a gesture or word to encourage your participation, then say:
   "Great! I'll play with the duck puppet."

4. If necessary, reinforce your actions with words. Comments to make include:
   "Ahmed, look at me. My hand is inside the puppet."
   "I can move the puppet because my hand is inside it."

5. Encourage the child to make the sound of the animal. Ask, for example:
   "Can you make a cow sound? Moo, moo."
   "What sound does a duck make? Quack, quack."

6. Reinforce the infant's animal noises by saying:
   "Ahmed, you mooed just like a cow!"
   "What a loud quack."

7. Model the animals having a conversation. Do this by having your puppet talk to the infant's puppet. This will foster the development of receptive language skills.

☀ Highlighting Development

A variety of tools such as puppets, stuffed animals, books, and cassettes all can be used to promote language skills in young children. Although children often show preferences for favorite tools, rotating them may introduce novelty, thus stimulating their interest.

VARIATION:

♡ Choose a book or books with the same animals as the puppets to read to the child.

ADDITIONAL INFORMATION:

♡ When purchasing books or puppets, choose those representing different ethnic groups.

♡ Choose puppets carefully. Because young children lack fine motor skills, the puppets need to be easy to manipulate.

♡ Puppets can also be used as a tool to encourage children to label items they touch.

10 to 12 months

Let's Play

Child's Developmental Goals

✓ To initiate a familiar game

✓ To practice using gestures to achieve a desired outcome

MATERIALS:

None

PREPARATION:

♡ Observe the child for her state of alertness.

NURTURING STRATEGIES:

1. While changing the infant's diaper, observe the behavioral cues being displayed such as the infant attempting to grab her toes.

2. Respond to the infant's cues. For example, say: *"Michaela, do you want to sing 'This Little Piggy'?"* Pause. Waiting for the infant to respond will display value and respect for the child.

3. If infant responds by shaking her head "no," bear in mind that children at this age are beginning to show negativity.

4. If infant responds "yes" by nodding, smiling, or otherwise showing interest, begin playing the game.

5. Throughout the interaction, keep smiling and showing interest. This nonverbal behavior will reinforce the infant for initiating the game.

6. When the game is over, reinforce the infant for initiating the game by making comments such as: *"Michaela, you picked a fun game to play."* *"What a great idea to play this game."*

7. If the infant shows interest by smiling, babbling, or maintaining eye contact, begin the game again.

☀ Highlighting Development

Infants use two forms of preverbal gestures to influence the behavior of others. The first is the protodeclarative, in which the infants touch, hold, or point to objects while looking at you to gain your attention. With the second type, called protoimperative, the infants get other people to do something by pointing, reaching, and often producing sounds at the same time (Bates, 1979; Fenson et al., 1994).

VARIATION:

♡ See Appendix D for a list of finger plays, nursery rhymes, and chants.

ADDITIONAL INFORMATION:

♡ As infants get older, they will begin initiating some of their favorite games with you. Careful observation will assist you in knowing what game they want to play.

♡ Following their lead shows infants that they do have an effect on their environment. In this way, it promotes their sense of self-efficacy.

10 to 12 months

Cognitive Development

TEN to TWELVE MONTHS

Ball and Tube

Child's Developmental Goals

✓ To refine the understanding of object permanence

✓ To continue developing cause-and-effect relationships

MATERIALS:

❑ 6 to 8 tennis balls
❑ 2 diaper pins
❑ 4-foot piece of hollow plastic tubing
❑ 2 twelve-inch pieces of elastic band
❑ 2 nonbreakable containers
❑ Masking tape

PREPARATION:

♡ Sand the ends of the plastic tubing to remove sharp edges.

♡ Choose a smooth area by a chain-link fence for this activity. If necessary, clear this area of debris.

♡ Align the pipe at an angle along the fence. The tip of the pipe should be between 2 and 3 feet from the ground, depending upon the height of the children. Secure the pipe to the fence using the elastic bands and diaper pins. Put one band at the top of the pipe and one at the bottom.

♡ Place one container at each end of the pipe. Put the tennis balls in the container under the tallest end. Adjust the placement of the container at the lower end. Check to ensure that when the tennis balls go through the tube, they land in the container.

NURTURING STRATEGIES:

1. When the activity is chosen, observe the child's behavior.

2. If the child appears to need help understanding the activity, verbally describe the activity. To illustrate, say:
   "Seiji, put the ball in the top. It will roll through the tube."

3. If necessary, reinforce your words with actions by putting the ball at the top of the tube and saying:
   "Seiji, put the ball in the tube."

4. To work on the concept of object permanence, ask the child:
   "Where did the ball go?"

5. Describe what happens after the child releases the tennis ball. Comments to make include:
   "Seiji, the ball rolls through the tube."
   "The ball lands in the container."
   These comments are important for assisting in development of cause-and-effect relationships.

6. Providing positive reinforcement may result in the child spending more time at the activity. Examples might include:
   "Seiji, you're working hard."
   "You like this game. You have a big smile on your face."

☀ Highlighting Development

Children at this stage are continuing to develop an understanding of object permanence. Objects out of sight are out of mind for the three-month-old child. By eight months, children begin searching for items that are covered. Now children's growth is evident. They will track and find toys that are covered.

VARIATION:

♡ Lower the height of the pipe so nonwalkers can do the activity while sitting on a blanket.

ADDITIONAL INFORMATION:

♡ If the children have not mastered the principle of object permanence, this game will have magical appeal.

 After closing diaper pins always secure them by wrapping in masking tape.

10 to 12 months

Which Are the Same?

Child's Developmental Goals

✓ To begin classifying objects

✓ To practice grouping similar objects

MATERIALS:

❑ 3 toys; 2 identical and 1 different such as 2 cars and 1 truck

PREPARATION:

♡ Select and clear an area that can be constantly supervised. Display the toys.

NURTURING STRATEGIES:

1. When the child selects the activity, observe the infant's behavior. Notice which toys the infant selects.
2. While the infant is playing, move closer and ask: *"Marya, which two toys are the same?"*
3. Reinforce the child's attempts or accomplishments at classifying the toys. Say, for example: *"That's right! There are two buses."* *"You pointed to a bus and a truck."*
4. Encourage the infant to physically separate the toys. To illustrate, while pointing say: *"Marya, put the buses over here and the truck over there."*
5. If necessary, reinforce your words with actions by moving the toys while saying: *"Put the buses together."*
6. Reinforce the child's attempts and accomplishments at separating the toys. Comments to make include: *"Marya, you put the buses together in one spot."* *"You separated the buses from the truck."*

☼ Highlighting Development

Classification is an important skill for young children (Herr, 1998). For infants at this age, classification is the process of physically grouping objects into categories or classes based upon unique features. Simple classification is the ability to group by color, size, or function. Language helps children categorize related objects because it provides the children with cues as to how items are alike and different from each other.

VARIATION:

♡ To challenge the infant, increase the number of objects to classify.

ADDITIONAL INFORMATION:

♡ Infants begin to classify objects very early in life. In fact, you have assisted them in acquiring these skills whenever you have described how toys are alike and different.

♡ The child's memory and visual perceptual skills are increasing. Both of these skills assist in making visual interpretations.

10 to 12 months

Which Box Is It In?

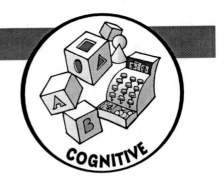

COGNITIVE

Child's Developmental Goals

✓ To refine the understanding of object permanence

✓ To remember where an object is hidden

✓ To use existing schemas to search for the hidden objects

MATERIALS:

❑ 2 boxes with lids

❑ 1 favorite toy that will fit inside both boxes

❑ Child-size table or coffee table

PREPARATION:

♡ Clean and sanitize the table. Set the two boxes and the toy on the table.

NURTURING STRATEGIES:

1. Invite the child to play a game with you. To illustrate, say:
   "Paolo, I have a game on the table. Want to play?"
2. When the child arrives at the table, pick up the toy. Explain the game by saying:
   "I'm going to hide the car in one of the boxes. You try to find it."
3. Hide the toy in a box. Say to the infant:
   "Find the car."
4. Provide positive reinforcement for attempts and accomplishments. Comments include:
   "Paolo, you did it; you found the cars."
   "You're looking in the box."
   "You lifted the lid and looked inside."

5. If the infant needs a challenge, hide the toy in one box and then move it to the other box while the infant is watching. Observe where the infant searches for the object.
6. Repeat the game as long as the infant seems interested.

☀ Highlighting Development

Understanding object permanence shows that the child is developing memory skills and goal-oriented thinking. Children at this stage of development typically have good memories. Their search strategies have matured. Watch them. Now they are able to follow the movement of an object from place to place.

VARIATION:

♡ Hide the toy in a gift bag or pillowcase.

ADDITIONAL INFORMATION:

♡ When infants search for the toy in a second hiding place, they are showing their understanding of object permanence.

Where Is It?

Child's Developmental Goals

✓ To search for a desired object

✓ To engage in intentional behaviors

MATERIALS:

❑ Child's security item(s) such as blanket, teddy bear, pacifier, etc.

PREPARATION:

♡ Place the security items in a convenient location.

NURTURING STRATEGIES:

1. When the child is upset, suggest locating a favorite comfort item. To illustrate, say:
   "Rylan, where is your doll? It helps you feel better to hug him."
   "Help me find your blanket. Where did you leave it?"

2. Suggest that the infant look for the item. Comments to say include:
   "Look. Where could it be? Move around the room."

3. Assist the infant in the search by suggesting where to look. Say, for example:
   "Rylan, you had your blanket at rest time. Look by your crib."
   "You were playing with your doll."

4. Provide positive reinforcement for attempts and accomplishments. Make comments such as:
   "Rylan, you remembered where you left your doll."
   "Keep looking. We'll find it soon."

☀ Highlighting Development

The role of the adult is to assist children in tasks beyond their skill level. This assistance can take the form of verbal or physical help. The term describing the adult's behavior when engaged in assisting the child is *scaffolding* (Vygotsky, 1978).

VARIATION:

♡ To promote memory skills, ask the infant to search for a lost toy.

ADDITIONAL INFORMATION:

♡ Assist infants in finding the lost item, especially when they are upset. The inability to remember is just as frustrating for young children as it is for adults.

Scavenger Hunt

COGNITIVE

Child's Developmental Goals

✓ To refine the understanding of object permanence

✓ To engage in intentional behaviors to solve a problem

MATERIALS:

❑ 1 set of star builder manipulatives

❑ Container to hold star builders

PREPARATION:

♡ Count and record the number of star builders in your set.

♡ Hide all but one of the star builder manipulatives either indoors or outdoors. See the Highlighting Development box.

♡ Put the remaining star builder in a pocket to show to the child later.

♡ Place the container in a central location.

NURTURING STRATEGIES:

1. Introduce the activity to the child. Using a tone that conveys enthusiasm, say:
   "I hid some star builders. Can you help me find them?"

2. Remove the star builder from your pocket while stating:
   "This is a star builder. Let's find them."

3. When the infant finds a hidden toy, either by crawling or walking to it, clap and verbally provide positive reinforcement. This may encourage the child to continue looking for the star builders. Comments include:
   "Benjamin, you found one!"
   "Wow! You are good at this game."

4. Explain the purpose of the container by saying:
   "Here is a special bucket. This bucket is for holding the star builders. Put the star builders in here."

5. If necessary, model putting the toy in the bucket by using the star builder you had in your pocket.

6. The child may need assistance in finding a hidden toy. Walk beside the infant while saying things such as:
   "Where could they be hiding? Let's look here by the chair."
   "Look behind the tree. You found one!"
   "Good work, Benjamin! Now, put the star builder in the bucket."

7. If the infant finds all the hidden toys and still is enjoying the game, you may want to continue by removing some of the star builders from the container and hiding them.

☀ Highlighting Development

Observe to note the child's understanding of object permanence. For some children at this stage, it is developmentally appropriate to completely hide the objects. For others, partially hidden objects are still a challenge to find. Therefore, you need to be aware of the child's developmental level to provide a stimulating, yet challenging, environment.

VARIATIONS:

♡ Hide items that are related but not identical such as plastic zoo or farm animals.

♡ Substitute by hiding large plastic blocks for a scavenger hunt.

ADDITIONAL INFORMATION:

♡ Children often enjoy finding their favorite toys.

♡ Evaluate the child's level of understanding of object permanence. Use that knowledge for hiding toys.

Sorting Cars

Child's Developmental Goals

✔ To distinguish objects that are different

✔ To categorize objects into two groups

MATERIALS:

☐ 6 red cars

☐ 6 blue cars

☐ Red bowl

☐ Blue bowl

☐ Clear container

☐ Child-size table or coffee table

PREPARATION:

♡ Clear an area on a child-size or coffee table. Place the cars in the clear container. Place one colored bowl on each side of the clear container.

NURTURING STRATEGIES:

1. When a child exhibits interest in the activity, introduce the activity by saying:
   "Tory, look at these cars."

2. Describe the toys to the infant. Comments to make include:
   "Here are red and blue cars."
   If necessary, say:
   "The cars are two different colors."

3. Observe the infant interacting with the toys. Ask yourself, "Is the infant sorting the cars by color?"

4. Suggest that the infant sort the cars. Say, for example:
   "Can you put the blue cars in the blue bowl?"
   "Can you divide the cars by color?"

5. Provide positive reinforcement for attempts or accomplishments. Comments include:
   "Tory, you did it. You put a red car in the red bowl."
   "You are sorting the cars."

☼ Highlighting Development

The development of a child's receptive and expressive language skills occurs at different rates. Receptive language or comprehension skills occur prior to expressive language skills, the ability to speak. Therefore, when describing the child's actions, you are building connections between actions and the spoken word. Infants may be able to sort by category; however, at this time they cannot tell us what they are doing or have done.

VARIATION:

♡ Use other objects for sorting.

ADDITIONAL INFORMATION:

♡ Avoid pushing the infants to sort items, even though they may exhibit this skill very early on. Suggest that they sort, but encourage free exploration of the materials.

10 to 12 months

A Visitor Comes

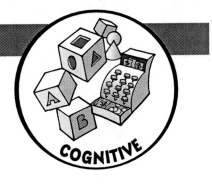
COGNITIVE

Child's Developmental Goals

✓ To distinguish strangers from familiar caregivers

✓ To cope with stranger anxiety

MATERIALS:

None

PREPARATION:

♡ If you know a visitor is coming, schedule his arrival after the child is well rested and fed.

NURTURING STRATEGIES:

1. When a stranger enters the room, greet the individual by saying:
   "Hello, Tres. How are you?"

2. Move closer to whomever may be experiencing stranger anxiety while saying in a calm, soothing voice:
   "Tres came to visit today."

3. If the child is becoming upset by the visitor's presence, talk about this so that both the visitor and the child understand it. Say, for example:
   "You don't remember Tres, do you? Tres is my friend. He visits us sometimes."

4. Your voice can be a tool for helping the child calm down. In addition, use your knowledge of the child when deciding on soothing techniques. Comments to make include:
   "Would you like to hold your ducky? It helps you to feel better."
   "Would you like me to rub your back? Rubbing helps you to calm down."

5. If the visitor seems upset by the child's reaction, explain that this is normal behavior for children this age.

☀ Highlighting Development

Once children begin grasping the concept of object permanence, they become frightened of unfamiliar faces. Typically this reaction occurs between 9 months and 15 months of age. After this period, the distress gradually weakens. Throughout this process, adults need to model and foster the development of successful coping skills to assist the child.

VARIATION:

♡ Slowly introduce children to adult strangers by taking walks in the community, taking them shopping, etc.

ADDITIONAL INFORMATION:

♡ Anticipate the child's reaction to strangers and be prepared to offer assistance to reduce anxiety.

Social Development

TEN to TWELVE MONTHS

All about Me

10 to 12 months

Child's Developmental Goals

✓ To recognize picture of self

✓ To recognize pictures of friends or family members

MATERIALS:

❏ Camera and film

❏ Tape

❏ Piece of paper with tree drawn on it

❏ Pictures of friends and family members, if available

PREPARATION:

♡ Take pictures of the child. If you are caring for more than one child, also take their pictures.

♡ Tape the pictures on the tree figure drawn on the piece of paper. Put the paper on a wall or bulletin board.

NURTURING STRATEGIES:

1. When a child observes the pictures, join the infant.
2. Watch the infant looking at or touching the pictures. It is typical for infants to try to remove the pictures. If you don't want the pictures removed, see the Variations section.
3. Talk to the infant about the pictures. For example, say:
   "Georgia, these are the children and teachers in this class."
4. Encourage the infant to find the picture of herself by asking:
   "Where is Georgia?"

5. Encourage the child to point to the picture by saying:
   "Point to the picture. Show me your picture."
6. Provide positive reinforcement for attempts or accomplishments. Comments might include:
   "Georgia, yes! That's you. You were eating in that picture."
   "You did it! You found your picture."
7. Repeat steps 4 to 6 by asking the child to find pictures of family members, if available.

☀ Highlighting Development

Gradually, children begin to recognize familiar people and objects in their world. When shown a photograph and people or objects are named, they will point to them. They will also use pointing to communicate their interest or to show recognition.

VARIATION:

♡ If desired, cover the paper with clear self-adhesive paper so that the pictures can be touched but not removed or damaged.

ADDITIONAL INFORMATION:

♡ Although infants are unable to recognize themselves in the mirror, they are beginning to recognize themselves in photographs. To develop a positive self-identity, activities like this are important.

SOCIAL

Playing in the Sand

Child's Developmental Goals

✓ To join a sibling or peer in play

✓ To play beside a sibling or peer

MATERIALS:

❑ A set of sand toys, including a bucket, scoop, and sieve, for each child you may be supervising

PREPARATION:

♡ Display the sand toys so they attract the infants' attention and suggest what materials belong to each child.

NURTURING STRATEGIES:

1. When a child chooses to play with the sand toys, move closer.
2. Observe the infant interacting/experimenting with the toys.
3. If possible, encourage another infant to join the first child in the sandbox by saying:
   "Loren, look at the sand toys. Would you like to dig?"
4. If the second child joins the area, comment on how the children are doing the same thing. To illustrate, say:
   "You two are both playing in the sand. Loren is digging and Jaden is filling the bucket."
   "You are both working in the sand area."
   "Loren is playing in the same area as Jaden."
5. If a sibling or peer is not available, join the activity.

Highlighting Development

Before learning to play with others, infants learn to play beside them. This is called parallel play. When engaged in parallel play, infants use similar materials as their playmates but have no verbal or visual interaction.

VARIATIONS:

♡ Use sand toys indoors in a plastic swimming pool or sensory table.

♡ Moisten the sand slightly to provide the children with another experience.

ADDITIONAL INFORMATION:

♡ Be proactive and introduce identical sets of materials. This reduces the potential for conflicts and makes conflicts that occur easier to solve. To illustrate, if a child takes another's scoop, say, "Here is your scoop."

♡ Sand play provides an opportunity for exploring different textures.

 Check the sand area for hazardous items such as broken glass or animal waste.

10 to 12 months

A Book about Me

SOCIAL

Child's Developmental Goals

✓ To develop a positive self-identity

✓ To recognize self in a photograph

MATERIALS:

❑ Camera and film

❑ Marker

❑ Construction paper

❑ Hole punch

❑ Yarn

❑ Glue

PREPARATION:

♡ Take and develop pictures of the child.

♡ Make a book of the child. To do this, cut the construction paper about 2 inches bigger than the photograph on all sides. To illustrate, if you have a 3-by-5-inch photo, cut the paper into 5-by-7-inch pieces. Cut a piece of paper for each picture. If possible, construct the covers from a heavier stock of paper. Glue one photograph on each page and allow to dry. Collate the pages of the book and the covers. Punch five to seven holes in the left-hand side of the book. Using yarn, lace the holes to bind the book, securing it with knots at both ends. Print "A Book about [child's name]" on the front cover and "The End" in the inside of the back cover.

NURTURING STRATEGIES:

1. Before nap time, place the book near the infant's crib or cot.

2. Read the book to the child before nap time. If the child likes to rock, read while rocking. If lying down is preferred, place the infant in the crib and rub the child's stomach while reading.

3. While reading the story, point to the pictures and say: "Who's this?"

4. Provide positive reinforcement for attempts and accomplishments. For example, say: "Yes, that is a picture of you. That is Corey."

5. Describe the pictures, pointing out activities the infant engages in. To illustrate, you may say: "Here you are pushing a truck. You like to push trucks and say 'voom, voom.'"
"It is nap time in this picture. You are hugging your baby and falling asleep. Just like now."

6. If the infant appears interested, read the story again.

☀ Highlighting Development

Infants can recognize pictures of themselves even though they are unable to recognize themselves in a mirror. Self-recognition refers to the perception of being a separate person, distinct from other people and objects in the surrounding environment. This process begins as early as the first few months of life but typically takes two years to fully develop. When provided with pictures or videotapes of their behavior, 9- to 12-month-old infants play peekaboo with their image (Berk, 1997).

VARIATIONS:

♡ Look at books of the infant's family, favorite toys, etc.

♡ Prepare books using pictures from toy catalogs.

ADDITIONAL INFORMATION:

♡ Use large, color photographs whenever possible.

♡ Books can be prepared for "My Favorite Toys," "My Friends," "My First Year of Life," "My Pets," etc.

Washing Babies

Child's Developmental Goals

✓ To begin to distinguish boys from girls
✓ To practice prosocial skills

MATERIALS:

❑ 1 large plastic quilt box
❑ 1 large towel
❑ Vinyl tablecloth
❑ Anatomically correct, multiethnic female and male doll
❑ 1 washcloth
❑ Smock or dry clothes

PREPARATION:

♡ Select and clear an area that can be constantly supervised. Then spread out the tablecloth.
♡ Fill the quilt box with 1 to 2 inches of warm water. Place the container on the tablecloth. Set both baby dolls inside. Place a washcloth on the edge of the container and place the towel on the tablecloth beside the container.
♡ If more than one child participates, individual materials should be provided for each.

NURTURING STRATEGIES:

1. When the child selects the activity, help the infant put on a smock. While introducing the activity, say, for example:
   "Eric, we are going to play in water. You can wash the baby."
2. Observe the infant's behavior with the baby. Encourage the infant to be gentle with the baby by saying:
   "Gently wash her face. She doesn't like water in her eyes."
   "You are washing his toes. Wash gently."

3. Help the child notice the differences in the ways the dolls look. For example, talk about the fact that one doll is female and one is a male. Also, discuss the differences in skin tones. Connect the doll's characteristics with the child's or family members'. To illustrate, say:
   "Eric, you have dark curly hair just like the doll."
   "This doll is a boy. You are also a boy."
4. Once the baby is washed, encourage the infant to dry it using the towel. In addition, you can suggest holding or cuddling the doll.
5. Reinforcing the infant's behaviors may promote the understanding of how to care for another. Comments may include:
   "Eric, you are taking care of the baby."
   "The baby was cold, so you're drying it."

☀ Highlighting Development

Infants this age are beginning to notice some basic biological differences between females and males. Using the correct language to label body parts is important. However, reinforce that there are more similarities than differences between the sexes.

VARIATION:

♡ To assist in developing body awareness, label the doll's parts. Begin with the most obvious such as eyes, arms, toes, legs, mouth, ears, and nose.

ADDITIONAL INFORMATION:

♡ All children need to be taught and reinforced for engaging in positive caregiving behaviors. Caring for others is an important skill children need to acquire.
♡ Children find playing with water a pleasurable sensory experience for learning about their environment.

Putting On Lotion

SOCIAL

Child's Developmental Goals

✓ To increase body awareness

✓ To interact with an adult

MATERIALS:

❑ Hand lotion with a pump dispenser

PREPARATION:

♡ Have the lotion in a convenient location, preferably on or near the sink.

NURTURING STRATEGIES:

1. After changing the infant's diaper, you and the infant need to wash your hands.
2. After washing your hands, encourage the infant to apply lotion. Say, for example:
   "Washing makes your hands dry. Would you like some lotion? Lotion keeps our hands soft."
   If the child responds "no," assist her in finding an activity. If the child responds "yes," retrieve the bottle of lotion.
3. Model dispensing the lotion. Connect your actions with words by saying, for example:
   "One push of lotion. Rub, rub, rub. I'm rubbing my hands together."
4. Encourage the infant to hold out her hands while dispensing lotion. Then say:
   "Rub your hands together. Spread out the lotion. Rub your fingers together!"
5. If necessary, reinforce your words with actions by rubbing the lotion on the child's hands while commenting:
   "Rub, rub, rub. I'm rubbing the lotion on your hands."

6. Providing positive reinforcement may encourage the infant to apply the lotion independently the next time. Comments to make include:
   "You rubbed on the lotion. Now your hands are soft."
   "We worked together to put lotion on your hands."

☀ Highlighting Development

An infant at this stage of development should be able to demonstrate knowledge of body parts. Recognition will be typically demonstrated through gestures such as pointing or showing. Labeling body parts throughout the first year of life assists children in developing this skill.

VARIATION:

♡ Encourage the infant to push the lotion lever independently.

ADDITIONAL INFORMATION:

♡ Always purchase nonfragrant, hypoallergenic lotion.

 Observe the infant carefully to make sure the lotion is not consumed orally. Avoid introducing this activity to children who suck their hands or fingers.

SOCIAL

Caring for Babies

Child's Developmental Goals

✓ To practice prosocial skills

✓ To play beside another child, if possible

MATERIALS:

❑ 2 anatomically correct, multiethnic female and male dolls

❑ 2 bottles

PREPARATION:

♡ Clear space on a child-size shelf for the dolls. Set the dolls on the shelf.

NURTURING STRATEGIES:

1. When a child begins interacting with the doll, observe the infant's behavior. Notice how the infant is caring for the doll.

2. Suggest new or different ways to care for the doll. For example, say:
   "Is the baby hungry? Does he need a bottle?"
   "Maybe the baby would like to rock in the rocking chair."
   "Would the baby like to go for a walk around the room?"

3. If another child is present, encourage playing with the dolls. To illustrate, say:
   "Jonah, would you like to feed this baby? She's hungry."
   "Hector, here is a baby for you."

4. If other children are present, discuss how the two children are playing with similar toys. Comments may include:
   "Charlene and Hector are both playing with dolls."
   "Jonah and Catherine are both feeding the babies."

5. Provide positive reinforcement for engaging in caregiving behaviors. For example, comment:
   "You are hugging the baby gently."
   "You help your baby. Your baby stopped crying."

☀ Highlighting Development

Children need to learn prosocial behavior, which includes acts of kindness toward others. These behaviors include helping, sharing, and cooperating. Examples include verbally and physically comforting others, cooperating at play and cleanup, sharing materials, showing concern, and sharing affection (Herr, 1998). Playing and caring for dolls can foster prosocial behavior.

VARIATION:

♡ Providing stuffed animals or puppets may also encourage caregiving behaviors.

ADDITIONAL INFORMATION:

♡ All children need to be taught how to care for others. These skills are the basis for future social skills such as empathy and perspective taking. All children, regardless of gender, need these skills.

♡ Whenever possible in guiding young children, use suggestions more than commands. Young children respond more positively to suggestions.

10 to 12 months

Chalk Scribbling

Child's Developmental Goals

✓ To play parallel to another child

✓ To engage in a conversation with another person

MATERIALS:

❑ 1 chalk set containing different colored pieces per child

❑ Nonbreakable container

PREPARATION:

♡ Select a section of the sidewalk out of the normal traffic path.

♡ Then place a container of chalk in the designated area. If other children join the activity, position them so there is working space.

NURTURING STRATEGIES:

1. To encourage chalk scribbling, sit by one of the containers. Your presence may gain the child's attention.

2. As the infant begins scribbling on the sidewalk, describe the child's actions. Comments to make include:
   "Isabel, you're making a long line with the red chalk."
   "Circles. You're drawing yellow circles."
   "Round and around your arm is going."

3. To engage the infant in conversation, ask questions. Your discussion may include events happening now, in the recent past, or in the near future. For example, say:
   "You like drawing."
   "You are making large markings."
   "We'll have a snack when we go inside. Would you like apples or oranges?"

4. Always provide the child with uninterrupted working time. Respond to vocalizations with positive nonverbal and verbal reinforcement. For example, nod your head and smile while saying:
   "Wow! I didn't know that. Tell me more."
   "Really! We'll have to make that snack."

5. If another child is present and joins the activity, provide a welcome by saying:
   "Would you like to draw with Isabel?"

6. Allow the children to work in silence together.

7. Comment on how the infants are using the same space and materials. Comments might include:
   "Isabel and Roslyn, you are both drawing with chalk. You are making a large picture."
   "Isabel is making big circles. Roslyn, you are making small circles. You're both drawing circles."

☀ Highlighting Development

First words tend to represent favorite people, objects that move, and familiar actions. Mostly children at this stage of development will use only one or two words to communicate. Later they will learn how to form sentences by forming a series of words. To understand the message they are communicating, observe their body language and listen to their vocalization.

VARIATION:

♡ This activity could be introduced indoors at a child-size table or coffee table. Cover the table with paper and provide the chalk.

ADDITIONAL INFORMATION:

♡ Your understanding of the conversation will depend on the infant's language skills. The social aspects of conversation are what is important rather than understanding the vocalizations.

Emotional Development

TEN to TWELVE MONTHS

Coming in from Outside

EMOTIONAL

10 to 12 months

Child's Developmental Goals

✓ To comply with a caregiver's request

✓ To assist in dressing self

MATERIALS:

☐ Children's clothing with large fasteners

PREPARATION:

♡ Dress the child with clothing containing large fasteners.

NURTURING STRATEGIES:

1. After coming in from outside, talk about what the infant needs to do before beginning to play. To illustrate, state:
   "Porter, you need to take off your coat. Then hang it up."

2. If necessary, assist the infant in unfastening the coat. Encourage the infant to help remove the coat by making comments such as:
   "Porter, pull them apart. Pull the snaps apart."

3. Reinforcing your words with actions may be necessary. If needed, open a snap and then encourage the infant to continue.

4. Provide positive reinforcement for attempts or accomplishments. To illustrate, say:
   "Thank you for helping, Porter."
   "What a helper! You opened your coat."

5. Once the coat is removed, say:
   "I am going to hang up your coat."

☀ Highlighting Development

Infants need lots of time to practice new skills. Being impatient or verbally pushing the child to work faster may result in the child refusing to help. Try fostering independence by being warm, nurturing, and patient when infants are learning or practicing these new skills. Always give the child the minimum amount of help, which will provide the maximum opportunity for independence.

VARIATION:

♡ Elicit the child's help when putting on the coat.

ADDITIONAL INFORMATION:

♡ Dressing can be a time-consuming and frustrating experience for an infant. Therefore, observe closely.

♡ If purchasing clothing for young children, select garments with fasteners that are large and, therefore, easy to manipulate.

♡ When the children's eye-hand and motor skills improve, they can use their fingers and hands to assist in dressing.

Pudding Time

Child's Developmental Goals

✓ To feed self using a spoon

✓ To express the emotion of excitement

MATERIALS:

❑ High chair or snack table
❑ Unbreakable bowls
❑ Spoon
❑ Bibs

PREPARATION:

♡ Prepare pudding from a mix or favorite recipe. Place the pudding in a small unbreakable bowl. Keep pudding refrigerated until snack time.

NURTURING STRATEGIES:

1. Before snack, warn the child that a transition is about to occur by saying:
   "It is almost snack time. We will need to wash our hands."
2. Before snack, bring out the pudding and place it out of reach.
3. Tell the child that it is time to go to the bathroom and wash hands. Assisting the child in this entire process will probably be necessary.
4. Help the child into a high chair or a seat at the snack table. To promote independence, offer the child a choice of two bibs. If needed, put the bib on the child.
5. Tell the children what is for snack by saying:
   "Today we have pudding for snack. You can eat it with a spoon."
6. Give the child a bowl and spoon.
7. Encourage the infant to use the spoon. Comments include:
   "Use your spoon."
   "Bring the pudding to your mouth with the spoon."

8. Providing positive reinforcement for attempts and accomplishments may result in the infant engaging in the behaviors again. For example, say:
   "Oh, it fell off. Try again."
   "You are working hard to use that spoon."
9. Comment on the infant's facial expressions, especially when the spoon reaches the mouth. To illustrate, say:
   "You are smiling. You must be excited about using the spoon."
   "You look excited. Is the pudding good?"

☀ Highlighting Development

At this stage, interest in self-feeding typically begins. Adults often have to assist the children in this process by helping them fill their spoon. Observe their manipulation of the eating tools. Because they lack coordination, they often turn the spoon before it reaches their mouths. Thus, the food on the spoon is dumped.

VARIATION:

♡ Other nutritious snacks such as applesauce or yogurt help the infant learn to use a spoon.

ADDITIONAL INFORMATION:

♡ Eating with a spoon can be a very frustrating experience. Often for infants, all the food falls off before it gets to the mouth! Therefore, encourage them to use the spoon but also discuss how using fingers can be efficient.

♡ Young children need to wear bibs because spilling occurs often.

 To avoid injuries caused by slipping, spilled food needs to be wiped up immediately.

10 to 12 months

Playing a Song

EMOTIONAL

Child's Developmental Goals

✓ To express feelings through music

✓ To initiate play with an adult

MATERIALS:

❑ 2 to 3 empty oatmeal or similar containers with lids

PREPARATION:

♡ Clean oatmeal containers and lids. Clear an area and place the containers where the child can view them.

NURTURING STRATEGIES:

1. When an infant chooses a container, observe the behavior.
2. If the infant initiates play with you by babbling or gazing, position yourself beside the child.
3. Describe the child's actions with the container. To illustrate, say:
   "Zoë, you're hitting the lid with your fingers."
   "You're using your palms to make music."
4. If a song comes to mind, sing it while the infant hits the drum.
5. If the infant seems interested in continuing, join the activity.
6. Imitate the infant's behaviors with the drum while commenting:
   "Zoë, look at me. I'm doing what you're doing."

7. Provide positive reinforcement for expressing feelings through music. Comment on the child's feelings at the time. Examples of comments include:
   "Zoë, you are playing a happy tune."
   "You are angry. You're hitting the drums very hard."

☀ Highlighting Development

Music can be used to help infants express their emotions. The role of the adult includes labeling the child's emotional expressions. Words to use include *happy, sad, excited, frustrated,* and *angry.*

VARIATIONS:

♡ Use other food containers such as nonbreakable peanut or some coffee containers. Listen. You will find that the sound generally varies with the size of the container.

♡ Choose a song in advance to accompany the drum.

ADDITIONAL INFORMATION:

♡ Infants enjoy making noise. At this stage, they have learned the principle of cause and effect. Consequently, providing them with appropriate outlets promotes independent play.

10 to 12 months

Getting Dressed

Child's Developmental Goals

✔ To increase knowledge of self-help skills

✔ To express happiness through clapping

MATERIALS:

☐ Cardboard book about dressing, such as *My Clothes* by Sian Tucker

PREPARATION:

♡ Recognize the child's readiness and interest in learning self-help skills.

♡ Place the book in an area that is easily accessible.

NURTURING STRATEGIES:

1. Gain the infant's attention by stating that you have a special book to read. See if the infant is interested in sitting on your lap. To illustrate, say:
   "Timothy, I have a special book about getting dressed. Would you like to sit in my lap while I read it?"

2. Begin reading the book. While pointing to each article of clothing, name it. Ask the child to point to a corresponding article of clothing on his body. For example, ask:
   "Where is your shirt?"
   "Where are my shoes?"

3. Provide positive reinforcement for attempts and accomplishments. Comments include:
   "Timothy, yes. That is your shirt."
   "Excellent!"
   "You are very good at this!"
   In addition, model clapping behaviors to show your excitement.

4. Discuss the similarities and differences in colors and styles of the infant's and your clothing. To illustrate, comment by saying:
   "Timothy, your shirt has buttons and mine has a zipper."
   "Your shoes are brown and mine are blue."
   "They are just like the ones in the book. You both have brown shoes."

5. If the infant shows interest, read the book again.

☀ Highlighting Development

Creating a stimulating environment for the infant is important. However, constant adult-child interaction can cause overstimulation and, therefore, stress. Observe the infants' signals. When infants become irritated, reduce the level of interaction. Like adults, children also need time to themselves.

VARIATION:

♡ To foster turn-taking skills, after you verbally identify and point to an article of clothing, encourage the child to repeat your behavior.

ADDITIONAL INFORMATION:

♡ For children to engage in self-help skills, they need to develop a working vocabulary. You can promote this development by providing a language-rich environment.

♡ Children at this stage typically use their two hands together symmetrically while clapping. When this occurs, both sides of the body are working together making the same motion at the same time.

10 to 12 months

"I Know an Old Turtle"

EMOTIONAL

Child's Developmental Goals

✓ To laugh in response to something funny

✓ To initiate playing with an adult

MATERIALS:

❏ Index card

❏ Felt–tip marker

PREPARATION:

♡ If desired, write out the words to the finger play on the index card.

NURTURING STRATEGIES:

1. When the infant approaches you, respond to the child's verbal and nonverbal cues. For example, say:
   "Do you want to play, Rory?" or
   "Well, hello Rory. Let's play."

2. Invite the child to sing a finger play with you by commenting:
   "You liked the finger play we did yesterday. Let's do it again."

3. Sing the finger play while performing the motions:

   ♫ I know an old turtle (fist)
   ♫ Who lives in a box (place fist on palm of other hand)
   ♫ Who swam in the puddles (swim fingers)
   ♫ And climbed on the rocks. (climb fingers upward)

   ♫ She snapped at a minnow (clap hands)
   ♫ She snapped at a flea (clap hands)
   ♫ She snapped at a mosquito (clap hands)
   ♫ She snapped at me! (clap hands)
   ♫ She caught the minnow (clap hands with arms extended, bring toward body)
   ♫ She caught the flea (clap hands with arms extended, bring toward body)
   ♫ She caught the mosquito (clap hands with arms extended, bring toward body)
   ♫ But she didn't catch me! (smile while shaking head no)

4. Respond to the infant's reactions to the finger play by describing what you observed. Comments to make include:
   "What a laugh. You like this finger play."
   "You smiled while clapping your hands. I think you like this song."

5. If the child seems interested, sing the finger play again.

☀ Highlighting Development

With familiar people, one-year-old children typically are friendly and social. At this stage of development, you need to continue playing, cuddling, hugging, rocking, singing, and talking to them. Through these actions, you are teaching children that they are loved, valued, and respected.

VARIATIONS:

♡ Substitute people or family names for bugs in the song.

♡ Sing a favorite song.

ADDITIONAL INFORMATION:

♡ Infants will often initiate contact with you. It is often difficult to understand their intentions. Do they want something specific or just your attention? Be prepared by having some finger plays or songs memorized for these occasions.

10 to 12 months

Solving Problems

Child's Developmental Goals

✓ To express emotions, such as anger

✓ To follow a caregiver's request or suggestion

MATERIALS:

❑ Pull toy

PREPARATION:

♡ Place the pull toy on a flat, smooth surface outdoors.

NURTURING STRATEGIES:

1. Observe the child interacting with a pull toy. When the pull toy falls over, the child may continue pulling but become frustrated and cry.
2. Walk over to the child and describe what you see. To illustrate, say:

   "Len, you are having trouble with the pull toy. You are crying because it won't work."
3. Ask the child a question to assist with the problem solving. For example, ask:

   "Is the pull toy working?"
4. If the child responds "no," respond by saying:

   "Len, set the toy on its wheels."

   If the child responds by saying "yes," then say:

   "Len, try it on the sidewalk."
5. When the child successfully pulls the toy on the sidewalk, provide positive reinforcement. Comments include:

   "You did it! You solved the problem! Now the toy works."

   "You figured out how to make the pull toy work."

Highlighting Development

Solving problems for infants fosters dependence rather than independence. Providing hints or suggestions allows them to discover the solution to the problems on their own, thereby promoting independence as well as positive self-esteem.

VARIATION:

♡ Note other sources of frustration for the child. Provide assistance and encouragement to allow the child to solve the problem.

ADDITIONAL INFORMATION:

♡ Observe the child and note when he is frustrated. Allow the infant time to experiment with possible solutions before offering assistance. This gives the child an opportunity to grow in independence.

♡ Provide the minimum amount of help to allow the infant the maximum learning experience.

♡ Pull toys are excellent for encouraging movement. They hold the child's attention while she is practicing walking. As they physically control a pull toy, children learn stop, go, and to change directions. Observe the child with the pull toy. With practice and experimentation, the child's interactions will become more refined.

10 to 12 months

Family Tree

10 to 12 months

Child's Developmental Goals

✓ To express excitement

✓ To clap when proud of self

MATERIALS:

❑ Pictures of the infant, the infant's family members, and pets

❑ Large sheet of paper

PREPARATION:

♡ Tape the pictures on a large piece of paper. Then tape the entire piece of paper onto a wall at the child's eye level. In a home environment, the pictures may be attached to the refrigerator or bulletin board, if desired.

NURTURING STRATEGIES:

1. When a child moves close to the pictures, join the infant.
2. Observe the infant looking at or touching the pictures. Typical behaviors include pointing, touching, and attempting to remove the pictures. This is normal behavior and should be encouraged.
3. Discuss the pictures with the infant. For example:
   "Janna, this is your picture. Look."
   "Here is your family."
4. Reinforce the infant's attempts and accomplishments. Say, for example:
   "You are excited! You're pointing to your grandma."
   "You did it! You pointed to your dog."

5. Model clapping as a way to show pride. For example, when the infant points to her family, clap while saying:
   "Janna, you should be proud. You found your daddy."

☀ Highlighting Development

At least two areas of development must be working at the same time for this experience to be successful. First, the infant must demonstrate the ability to retrieve information stored in her long-term memory by recognizing a familiar face. This recognition, then, results in an emotional reaction such as happiness.

VARIATIONS:

♡ To allow the infant repeated exposure, preserve the collage of pictures. Cover the entire paper in a clear, self-adhesive laminate so that the pictures can be touched but not damaged or removed.

♡ Extend the activity by cutting pictures from magazines, catalogs, and calendars of animals, transportation vehicles, and clothing to create concept pictures.

ADDITIONAL INFORMATION:

♡ Changing the pictures over time will create interest. Moreover, it depicts changes in the child's and family's development.

Abrams, B. W., & Kaufman, N. A. (1990). *Toys for early childhood development*. West Nyack, NY: The Center for Applied Research in Education.

Bates, E. (1979). *The emergence of symbols: Cognition and communication in infancy*. New York: Academic Press.

Bentzen, W. R. (2001). *Seeing young children: A guide to observing and recording behavior* (4th ed.). Clifton Park, NY: Delmar Learning.

Berk, L. E. (1997). *Child development* (4th ed.). Boston: Allyn & Bacon.

Black, J. K., & Puckett, M. B. (1996). *The young child: Development from prebirth through age eight* (2nd ed.). Englewood Cliffs, NJ: Prentice Hall.

Bukato, D., & Daehler, M. W. (1995). *Child development: A thematic approach*. Boston: Houghton Mifflin.

Butterworth, G. (1997). Starting point. *Natural History, 106* (4), 14–16.

Feldman, R. S. (1998). *Child Development*. Upper Saddle River, NJ: Prentice Hall.

Fenson, L., Dale, P. S., Reznick, J. S., Bates, E., Thal, D. J., & Pethick, S. J. (1994). Variability in early communication development. *Monographs of the Society for Research in Child Development, 59* (5, Serial No. 242).

Herr, J. (1998). *Working with young children*. Homewood, IL: Goodheart-Wilcox.

Leach, P. (1992). *Your baby and child: From birth to age five*. New York: Alfred A. Knopf.

Shore, R. (1997). *Rethinking the brain: New insights into early development*. New York: Families and Work Institute.

Snow, C. W. (1998). *Infant development* (2nd ed.). Upper Saddle River, NJ: Prentice Hall.

Vygotsky, L. S. (1978). *Mind in society: The development of higher mental processes*. Cambridge, MA: Harvard University Press. (Original works published 1930, 1933, and 1935)

Books for Infants

Young children need to be immersed in a literacy-rich environment. A foundation for reading success begins as early as the first few months of life. Exposure to books and caring adults nourishes literacy development. Books and oral language are tools to help infants become familiar with language. Young children enjoy handling books and listening to stories. Infants enjoy the visual and auditory stimulation of having books read to them over and over again.

Books help very young children by:

♡ Developing visual discrimination skills

♡ Developing visual memory skills

♡ Developing listening skills

♡ Developing auditory memory skills

♡ Presenting new and interesting information

♡ Introducing new vocabulary

♡ Stimulating new thoughts and ideas

♡ Helping children learn book-handling skills such as turning pages and reading text versus pictures

Books that are developmentally appropriate for infants are abundant. Some of the best examples feature various physical formats combined with clearly developed concepts or a simple story and distinctive art or photographic work.

Features of books for babies and infants include a scaled-down size appropriate for manipulation with small hands and for lap reading. Pages are either soft for safety or thick for sturdiness and ease of turning. Many books have a wipe-clean finish and rounded corners for safety. Formats include cloth, vinyl, and floatable bathtub books in chunky sizes. The content is concept-oriented with clear pictures or photographs, usually including babies or objects relating to a baby's life.

SELECTING BOOKS

Careful consideration should be given to selecting age-appropriate books for young children. When choosing books, begin by looking for award winners. You can ask the librarian at your local library to give you a list of award-winning picture books; likewise, do not hesitate to ask the salesperson at a local bookstore to provide this information. Chances are they will have a list of these award-winning books or can complete a computer search to obtain this information for you. On-line merchants should also be able to provide you this information.

You should also review the illustrations for size and quality before selecting a picture book. Study them carefully. You will notice a wide variety of illustration types in books for infants. There are photographs, watercolors, line drawings, and collages. As you review books, remember that infants need to have large, realistic illustrations. Realistic illustrations serve two purposes: They help the young children maintain their interest in the book and they help develop concept formation.

Other questions beside award-winning status and quality of illustrations to ask yourself while evaluating books for infants include:

♡ Is the book developmentally appropriate for the child or group of children?

♡ Does the book have visual appeal?

♡ Are the pages thick, durable, and easy to clean?

♡ Are the illustrations large and brightly colored?

♡ Do the illustrations contain pictures of familiar objects, routines, or people?

♡ Does the story reflect the children's own experiences?

♡ Is the vocabulary appropriate?

SUGGESTIONS FOR READING TO INFANTS

There are seven steps to making reading an enjoyable and educational experience for infants.

♡ Get comfortable! Sit on a couch, in a rocking chair, or on the floor with your back against a wall. Hold the child in your lap or snuggle close to a small group of children.

♡ Read slowly, allowing plenty of time for children to look at the illustrations. This increases the pleasure and enjoyment derived from books for *everyone* involved.

♡ Ask questions to engage children in conversation. The experience should be as much about speaking skills as listening skills for young children.

♡ Pause to encourage children to read along with you. You will find that infants will coo or babble. These experiences also serve to reinforce the development of turn-taking skills.

♡ Follow their lead. For example, encourage children to turn the pages. Do not worry if pages are skipped. It is highly likely that whatever you miss now will be covered in future readings of the book.

♡ Read for as long as children enjoy it. Forcing young children to remain in a situation when they are finished only serves to diminish their "love of books."

♡ Share your enthusiasm for the book through your voice and facial expressions. Children learn to love books when an adult shares their own enjoyment.

CLOTH BOOKS

Animal Play. Dorling Kindersley, 1996.

Briggs, Raymond. *The Snowman.* Random House, 1993.

Cousins, Lucy. My First Cloth Book series. Candlewick Press.
  Flower in the Garden. 1992.
  Hen on the Farm. 1992.
  Kite in the Park. 1992.
  Teddy in the House. 1992.

Harte, Cheryl. *Bunny Rattle.* Random House, 1989. (Has a rattle in it)
  Ducky Squeak. Random House, 1989. (Has a squeaker in it)

Hill, Eric. *Clothes-Spot Cloth Book.* Putnam, 1993.
  Play-Spot Cloth Book. Putnam, 1993.

My First Notebook. Eden International Ltd. (Has a rattle inside and plastic spiral rings.)

Pienkowski, Jan. Jan Pienkowski's First Cloth Book series. Little Simon.
  Animals. 1995.
  Friends. 1995.
  Fun. 1996.
  Play. 1995.

Pienkowski, Jan. *Bronto's Brunch.* Dutton Books, 1995. (Has detachable pieces. Ages 3+)
  Good Night, Moo. Dutton Books, 1995. (Has detachable pieces. Ages 3+)

Potter, Beatrix. Beatrix Potter Cloth Books. Frederick Warne & Co.
  My Peter Rabbit Cloth Book. 1994.
  My Tom Kitten Cloth Book. 1994.

Pudgy Pillow Books. Grosset & Dunlap.
  Baby's Animal Sounds. 1989.
  Baby's Little Engine That Could. 1989.
  Barbaresi, Nina. *Baby's Mother Goose.* 1989.
  Ulrich, George. *Baby's Peek A Boo.* 1989.

Tong, Willabel L. Cuddly Cloth Books. Andrews & McMeel.
  Farm Faces. 1996.
  My Pets. 1997.
  My Toys. 1997.
  Zoo Faces. 1997.

Tucker, Sian. My First Cloth Book series. Simon & Schuster.
  Quack, Quack. 1994.
  Rat-A-Tat-Tat. 1994.
  Toot Toot. 1994.
  Yum Yum. 1994.

VINYL COVER AND BATH BOOKS

Bracken, Carolyn. *Baby's First Rattle: A Busy Bubble Book.* Simon & Schuster, 1984.

De Brunhoff, Laurent. *Babar's Bath Book.* Random House, 1992.

Hill, Eric. *Spot's Friends.* Putnam, 1984.
  Spot's Toys. Putnam, 1984.
  Sweet Dreams, Spot. Putnam, 1984.

Hoban, Tana. *Tana Hoban's Red, Blue, Yellow Shoe.* Greenwillow Books, 1994.
  Tana Hoban's What Is It? Greenwillow Books, 1994.

I. M. Tubby. *I'm a Little Airplane.* Simon & Schuster, 1982. (Shape book)
  I'm a Little Choo Choo. Simon & Schuster, 1982. (Shape book)
  I'm a Little Fish. Simon & Schuster, 1981. (Shape book)

My First Duck. Dutton, 1996. (Playskool shape book)

Nicklaus, Carol. *Grover's Tubby.* Random House/ Children's Television Workshop, 1992.

Potter, Beatrix. Beatrix Potter Bath Books series. Frederick Warne & Co.
  Benjamin Bunny. 1994.
  Jemima Puddle-Duck. 1988.
  Mr. Jeremy Fisher. 1989.
  Peter Rabbit. 1989.
  Tom Kitten, Mittens, and Moppet. 1989.

Reichmeier, Betty. *Potty Time.* Random House, 1988.

Smollin, Michael J. *Ernie's Bath Book.* Random House/ Children's Television Workshop, 1982.

Tucker, Sian. Sian Tucker Bath Books series. Simon & Schuster.
  Animal Splash. 1995.
  Splish Splash. 1995.

TOUCH AND FEEL BOOKS

Carter, David A. *Feely Bugs.* Little Simon, 1995.

Chang, Cindy. *Good Morning Puppy.* Price Stern Sloan, 1994.
  Good Night Kitty! Price Stern Sloan, 1994.

Demi, Hitz. *Downy Duckling.* Grosset & Dunlap, 1988.
  Fluffy Bunny. Grosset & Dunlap, 1987.

Hanna, Jack. *Let's Go to the Petting Zoo with Jungle Jack.* Doubleday, 1992.

Hill, Eric. *Spot's Touch and Feel Day.* Putnam, 1997.

Kunhardt, Dorothy. *Pat the Bunny.* Western Publishing, 1968.

Kunhardt, Dorothy & Edith. *Pat the Cat.* Western Publishing, 1984.
  Pat the Puppy. Western Publishing, 1993.

Lodge, J. *Patch and His Favorite Things.* Harcourt Brace, 1996.
  Patch in the Garden. Harcourt Brace, 1996.

Offerman, Lynn. *Puppy Dog's Special Friends.* Joshua Morris Publishing, 1998.

Scarry, Richard. *Richard Scarry's Egg in the Hole Book.* Golden Books, 1997.

Witte, Pat & Eve. *The Touch Me Book.* Golden Books, 1946.

CHUNKY AND CHUBBY BOOKS

Barton, Byron. Chunky Board Book series. HarperCollins.
Boats. 1994.
Planes. 1994.
Trains. 1994.

Bond, Michael. *Paddington at the Seashore.* HarperCollins, 1992.

Brown, Marc. Chunky Flap Book series. Random House.
Arthur Counts. 1998.
Arthur's Farm Tales. 1998.
D. W.'s Color Book. 1997.
Where Is My Frog? 1991.
Where's Arthur's Gerbil? 1997.
Where's My Sneaker? 1991.

Cowley, Rich. *Snap! Snap! Buzz Buzz.* Firefly Books, 1996.

Dunn, Phoebe. *Baby's Animal Friends.* Random House, 1988.
Farm Animals. Random House, 1984.

Freeman, Don. *Corduroy's Toys.* Viking, 1985.

Fujikawa, Gyo. *Good Night, Sleep Tight! Shhh . . .* Random House, 1990. (Chunky shape)

Hill, Eric. Spot Block Book series. Putnam.
Spot's Favorite Baby Animals. 1997.
Spot's Favorite Numbers. 1997.
Spot's Favorite Words. 1997.

Hirashima, Jean. *ABC.* Random House, 1994. (Chunky shape)

Ingle, Annie. *Zoo Animals.* Random House, 1992.

Loehr, Mallory. *Trucks.* Random House, 1992. (Chunky shape)

Marzollo, Jean. *Do You Know New?* HarperCollins, 1997.

McCue, Lisa. *Little Fuzzytail.* Random House, 1995. (Chunky Peek a Board Book)

Miller, Margaret. Super Chubby Book series. Simon & Schuster.
At the Shore. 1996.
Family Time. 1996.
Happy Days. 1996.
Let's Play. 1997.
My Best Friends. 1996.
Water Play. 1996.
Wheels Go Round. 1997.

Oxenbury, Helen. *Helen Oxenbury's Little Baby Books.* Candlewick Press, 1996.
Boxed set includes: *I Can; I Hear; I See; I Touch.*

Pienkowski, Jan. Nursery Board Book series. Simon & Schuster.
Colors. 1987.   *Sizes.* 1991.
Faces. 1991.   *Stop Go.* 1992.
Food. 1991.   *Time.* 1991.
Homes. 1990.   *Yes No.* 1992.

Ricklen, Neil. Super Chubby Book series. Simon & Schuster.
Baby Outside. 1996.   *Baby's Good Night.* 1992.
Baby's 123. 1990.   *Baby's Neighborhood.* 1994.
Baby's ABC. 1997.   *Baby's Playtime.* 1994.
Baby's Big & Little. 1996.   *Baby's Toys.* 1997.
Baby's Clothes. 1997.   *Baby's Zoo.* 1992.
Baby's Friends. 1997.   *Daddy and Me.* 1997.
Baby's Home. 1997.   *Mommy and Me.* 1997.
Baby's Good Morning. 1992.

Ross, Anna. *Knock Knock, Who's There?* Random House/Children's Television Workshop, 1994. (Chunky flap)

Ross, Katharine. *The Little Quiet Book.* Random House, 1989.

Santoro, Christopher. *Open the Barn Door.* Random House, 1993. (Chunky flap)

Scarry, Richard. *Richard Scarry's Lowly Worm Word Book.* Random House, 1981.
Richard Scarry's Cars and Trucks from A–Z. Random House, 1990. (Chunky shape)

Shappie, Trisha Lee. *Where Is Your Nose?* Scholastic, 1997.

Smollin, Michael. *In & Out, Up & Down.* Random House, Children's Television Network, 1982.
Ernie & Bert Can . . . Can You? Random House, Children's Television Network, 1982.

Snapshot Chubby Book series. Dorling Kindersley.
ABC. 1994.
Colors. 1994.
My Home. 1995.
My Toys. 1995.
Shapes. 1994.

Van Fleet, Matthew. *Fuzzy Yellow Ducklings.* Dial Books, 1995.

Wik, Lars. *Baby's First Words.* Random House, 1985.

BOARD BOOKS

Alborough, Jez. *Ice Cream Bear.* Candlewick Press, 1997.
It's the Bear. 1994.
My Friend Bear. 1998.
Bare Bear. Random House, 1984.
Running Bear. 1985.

Bang, Molly. *Ten, Nine, Eight.* First Tupelo Board Book edition. Tupelo Books, 1998.

Boynton, Sandra. Boynton Board Book series. Simon & Schuster.
But Not the Hippopotamus. 1995.
Blue Hat, Green Hat. 1995.
Doggies, A Counting and Barking Book. 1995.
Going to Bed Book. 1995.
Moo, Baa, La La La. 1995.
Opposites. 1995.
Hey! Wake Up! Workman Publishing, 2000.

Brett, Jan. *The Mitten: A Ukrainian Folktale.* Putnam, 1996. (Board book)

Brown, Margaret Wise. First Board Book editions. HarperCollins.
Child's Good Night Book. Pictures by Jean Charlot. 1996.
Goodnight Moon. Pictures by Clement Hurd. 1991.
Runaway Bunny. Pictures by Clement Hurd, 1991.

Carle, Eric. First Board Book editions. HarperCollins.
Do You Want to Be My Friend? 1995.
The Mixed-Up Chameleon. 1998.
The Secret Birthday Message. 1998.
The Very Quiet Cricket. Putnam, 1997.
Have You Seen My Cat? First Little Simon Board Book edition. Simon & Schuster, 1996.
The Very Hungry Caterpillar. First Board Book edition. Philomel Books, 1994.

Carle, Eric. Play-and-Read Books. Cartwheel Books.
Catch the Ball. 1998.
Let's Paint a Rainbow. 1998.
What's for Lunch? 1998.

Carlstrom, Nancy White. Illus. by Bruce Degen. Simon & Schuster. (Board book)
Bizz Buzz Chug-A-Chug: Jesse Bear's Sounds. 1997.
Hooray for Blue: Jesse Bear's Colors. 1997.
I Love You, Mama, Any Time of Year. Jesse Bear Board Book. 1997.
I Love You, Papa, In All Kinds of Weather. Jesse Bear Board Book. 1997.
Jesse Bear, What Will You Wear? 1996.

Choosing Colors. Photos by Sandra Lousada. Dutton Children's Books/Playskool, 1995. (Board book)

Cohen, Miriam. *Backpack Baby.* Star Bright Books, 1999.
Say Hi, Backpack Baby: A Backpack Baby Story. 2000.

Cousins, Lucy. Dutton Children's Books. (Board book)
Humpty Dumpty and Other Nursery Rhymes. 1996.
Jack & Jill and Other Nursery Rhymes. 1996.
Little Miss Muffet and Other Nursery Rhymes. 1997.
Wee Willie Winkie and Other Nursery Rhymes. 1997.

Day, Alexandra. *Good Dog, Carl.* First Little Simon Board Book edition. Simon & Schuster, 1996.

Degen, Bruce. *Jamberry.* First Board Book edition. HarperCollins, 1995.

dePaola, Tomie. *Strega Nona.* First Little Simon Board Book edition. Simon & Schuster, 1997.

Ehlert, Lois. *Color Farm.* First Board Book edition. HarperCollins, 1997.
Color Zoo. First Board Book edition. HarperCollins, 1997.
Eating the Alphabet. First Red Wagon Books. Harcourt Brace, 1996.

Fleming, Denise. *Count!* First Board Book edition. Henry Holt, 1997.
Mama Cat Has Three Kittens. 1998.
The Everything Book. 2000.

Hoban, Tana. *Black on White.* Greenwillow Books, 1993.
Red, Blue, Yellow Shoe. 1986.

What Is It? 1985.
White on Black. 1993.

Hooker, Yvonne. Illus. by Carlo A. Michelini. Poke and Look books. Grosset & Dunlap.
One Green Frog. 1989.
Wheels Go Round. 1989.

Hopp, Lisa. *Circus of Colors.* Illus. by Chiara Bordoni. Poke and Look book. Grosset & Dunlap, 1997.

Isadora, Rachel. *I Touch.* Greenwillow Books, 1991. (Board book)

Keats, Ezra Jack. *The Snowy Day.* Viking, 1996. (Board book)

Kirk, David. *Miss Spider's Tea Party: The Counting Book.* First Board Book edition. Callaway & Kirk/Scholastic Press, 1997.

Lewison, Wendy. *Nighty Night.* Illus. by Giulia Orecchia. Poke and Look book. Grosset & Dunlap, 1992.

Lundell, Margaretta. *Land of Colors.* Illus. by Nadia Pazzaglia. Poke and Look book. Grosset & Dunlap, 1989.

Lundell, Margo. *What Does Baby See?* Illus. by Roberta Pagnoni. Poke and Look book. Putnam & Grosset, 1990.

Martin, Bill. Illus. by Eric Carle. First Board Book editions. Henry Holt.
Brown Bear, Brown Bear, What Do You See? 1996.
Polar Bear, Polar Bear, What Do You Hear? 1997.

Martin, Bill, & Archambault, John. *Chicka Chicka ABC.* Illus. by Lois Ehlert. First Little Simon Board Book edition. Simon & Schuster, 1993.

Marzollo, Jean. *I Spy Little Book.* Illus. by Walter Wick. Scholastic, 1997. (Board book)
I Spy Little Animals. Photos by Walter Wick. 1998. (Board book)
Do You Know New? HarperCollins, 1997.
Mama, Mama. HarperFestival, 1999.
Papa, Papa. 2000.
Pretend You're a Cat. Dial Books, 1990.

McBratney, Sam. *Guess How Much I Love You.* First Board Book edition. Candlewick Press, 1996.

McMullan, Kate. *If You Were My Bunny.* Illus. by David McPhail. First Board Book edition. Cartwheel Books, 1998.

Miller, Margaret. *Baby Faces.* Little Simon, 1998.
What's On My Head? 1998.

Miller, Virginia. *Be Gentle!* Candlewick Press, 1997.
Eat Your Dinner! 1992.
Go to Bed! 1993.
In a Minute! 2000.
On Your Potty! 1998.

Ogden, Betina, illus. *Busy Farmyard.* So Tall board book. Grosset & Dunlap, 1995.

Omerod, Jan. *101 Things to Do With a Baby.* Mulberry Books, 1993.

Opie, Iona Archibald. Illus. by Rosemary Wells. Mother Goose Board Book series. Candlewick Press.
Pussycat, Pussycat and Other Rhymes. 1997.
Humpty Dumpty and Other Rhymes. 1997.

Little Boy Blue and Other Rhymes. 1997.

Wee Willie Winkie and Other Rhymes. 1997.

Oxenbury, Helen. Baby Board Books. Wanderer Books.

Dressing. 1981.

Family. 1981.

Friends. 1981.

Playing. 1981.

Working. 1981.

Pfister, Marcus. Board book. North-South Books.

Hopper. 1998.

Hopper Hunts for Spring. 1998.

The Rainbow Fish. 1996.

Rainbow Fish to the Rescue. 1998.

Pinkney, Andrea & Brian. *Pretty Brown Face.* Harcourt Brace, 1997.

Piper, Watty. *The Little Engine That Could.* Illus. by Christina Ong. Platt & Munk, 1991.

Potter, Beatrix. *The Tale of Peter Rabbit.* Illus. by Florence Graham. Pudgy Pal Board Book. Grosset & Dunlap, 1996.

Pragoff, Fiona. Fiona Pragoff Board Books. Simon & Schuster.

Baby Days. 1995.

Baby Plays. 1995.

Baby Ways. 1994.

It's Fun to Be One. 1994.

It's Fun to Be Two. 1994.

Raffi. First Board Book editions. Crown Publishers.

Baby Beluga. Illus. by Ashley Wolff. 1997.

Wheels on the Bus. Illus. by Sylvie Kantorovitz Wickstrom. 1998.

Rathmann, Peggy. *Good Night, Gorilla.* Board book. Putnam, 1996.

Reasoner, Charles, & Hardt, Vicky. *Alphabite! A Funny Feast from A to Z.* Board book. Price Stern Sloan, 1989.

Rey, H. A. & Margret. Board books. Houghton Mifflin, 1998.

Curious George and the Bunny. 1998.

Curious George's ABC's. 1998.

Curious George's Are You Curious? 1998.

Curious George's Opposites. 1998.

Rosen, Michael. *We're Going on a Bear Hunt.* Illus. by Helen Oxenbury. First Little Simon Board Book edition. Simon & Schuster, 1997.

Seuss, Dr. Bright and Early Board Book series. Random House.

Dr. Seuss's ABC. 1996.

The Foot Book. 1997.

Mr. Brown Can Moo, Can You? 1996.

The Shape of Me and Other Stuff. 1997.

There's a Wocket in My Pocket. 1996.

Snapshot Board Book series. Dorling Kindersley.

All about Baby by Stephen Shott. 1994.

Baby and Friends by Paul Bricknell. 1994.

Good Morning, Baby by Jo Foord, et al. 1994.

Good Night, Baby by Mike Good & Stephen Shott. 1994.

Waddell, Martin. *Owl Babies.* Illus. by Patrick Benson. First Board Book edition. Candlewick Press, 1992.

Wells, Rosemary. *Max's Birthday.* Max Board Book. Dial Books for Young Readers, 1998.

Old MacDonald. Bunny Reads Back Board Book. Scholastic, 1998.

Wilkes, Angela. *My First Word Board Book.* Dorling Kindersley, 1997.

Williams, Sue. *I Went Walking.* Illus. by Julie Vivas. First Red Wagon Books edition. Harcourt Brace, 1996.

Williams, Vera B. *More, More, More Said the Baby.* First Tupelo Board Book edition. William Morrow, 1997.

Wood, Jakki. *Moo Moo, Brown Cow.* Illus. by Rog Bonner. First Red Wagon Board book. Harcourt Brace, 1996.

Ziefert, Harriet. Board Book. Dorling Kindersley.

Food! 1996.

Let's Get Dressed. Illus. by Susan Baum. 1997.

My Clothes. 1996.

Criteria for Selecting Materials and Equipment for Children

Even though most materials and equipment appear safe, you will find that infants have an uncanny ability to find and remove parts. This may pose a threat. Therefore, to reduce safety hazards, you must constantly check and observe. When purchasing or choosing materials and equipment to use with infants, carefully determine if the items promote safety and development by using the following checklist.

SAFETY	Yes	No
A. Is it unbreakable?		
B. Is it durable?		
C. Is it washable?		
D. Is it too large to be swallowed?		
E. Is it free of removable parts?		
F. Is it free of sharp edges?		
G. Is it constructed from nontoxic materials?		
H. Is it free of pinching cracks?		
I. Is it suitable for the available space?		
PROMOTES DEVELOPMENT		
A. Is it developmentally appropriate?		
B. Does it challenge the child's development?		
C. Does it complement existing materials or equipment?		
D. Does it teach multiple skills?		
E. Does it involve the child?		
F. Is it nongender biased?		
G. Does it promote a multicultural perspective?		
H. Does it promote nonviolent play?		

Materials and Equipment for Promoting Optimal Development

Materials and equipment play a major role in promoting an infant's development, as well as provide enjoyment.

Materials and Equipment to Promote Development for Infants

animal, toy
baby lotion
balls
bells
blanket or mat
blocks for building, lightweight
books (black & white and picture books—cardboard, cloth, and/or vinyl)
carpet pieces
cars, large toy
cassettes or compact discs, a variety of music: jazz, lullabies, classical, etc.
couch or sturdy furniture
crayons, large
diaper-changing table
dishes, nonbreakable (e.g., cups, spoons, plates)
doll accessories: blanket, bed, clothes

dolls, multiethnic
doughs and clays
elastic bands
fill and dump toys
glider
high chair
household items (e.g., pots, pans, wooden spoons, metal or plastic bowls, laundry baskets)
infant seat
infant stroller
large beads to string
mirrors (unbreakable)
mobile
musical instruments, child-size
nesting cups
pacifier
pails and shovels
paintbrushes
pictures of infants
pillows

pop-up toys
props to accompany finger plays
puppets
puzzles with large pieces
push and pull toys
rattles, different sizes, shapes, weights, and textures
riding toys
rocking chair
rubber toys
squeeze toys
stacking rings
stroller
stuffed animals
sun catchers
tape or compact disc recorder
teething rings
towels
toy telephones
wheeled toys
wind chimes

Favorite Finger Plays, Nursery Rhymes, and Chants

Finger plays, nursery rhymes, and chants help infants to develop social interaction skills, listening and auditory memory skills, expressive language skills, and concept formation. They also help infants become aware of their body parts and see themselves as persons who can do things.

Finger plays use a variety of actions and words together; some involve whole body actions. An example is the finger play "This Little Piggy," which is a favorite for infants. The younger the child, the shorter and simpler the rhyme and the body action need to be. For these children, larger body parts are more suitable. The young child will join you visually and participate in the actions before learning the words. This appendix contains examples of finger plays, nursery rhymes, and chants that children may enjoy. Note that finger plays can be an important technique for teaching "Who am I?"; young children particularly enjoy these activities when their names are included.

ANIMALS

Can you hop like a rabbit?
   (*suit actions to words*)
Can you jump like a frog?
Can you walk like a duck?
Can you run like a dog?
Can you fly like a bird?
Can you swim like a fish?
And be still like a good child?
As still as this?

BODY TALK

When I smile, I tell you that I'm happy.
   (*point to the mouth*)
When I frown I tell you that I am sad.
   (*pull down corners of the mouth*)
When I raise my shoulders and tilt my head I tell you,
   "I don't know."
(*raise shoulders, tilt head, raise hands, and shake head*)

BRUSHING TEETH

I move the toothbrush back and forth.
   (*pretend to brush teeth*)
I brush all of my teeth.
I swish the water to rinse them and then
   (*puff out cheeks to swish*)
I look at myself and smile.
   (*smile at one another*)

THE CHIMNEY

Here is the chimney,
   (*make hand into a fist with thumb inside*)
Here is the top.
   (*place other hand on top of fist*)

Open the lid.
   (*remove top hand*)
Out Santa will pop.
   (*pop up thumb*)

A CIRCLE

Around in a circle we will go.
Little tiny baby steps make us go very slow.
And then we'll take some great giant steps,
As big as they can be.
Then in a circle we'll stand quietly.

CIRCUS CLOWN

I'd like to be a circus clown
And make a funny face,
   (*make a funny face*)
And have all the people laugh at me
As I jump around the place.
   (*act silly and jump around*)

CLAP YOUR HANDS I

Clap your hands 1, 2, 3.
   (*suit actions to words*)
Clap your hands just like me.
Roll your hands 1, 2, 3.
Roll your hands just like me.

CLAP YOUR HANDS 2

Clap, clap, clap your hands,
As slowly as you can.
Clap, clap, clap your hands,
As fast as you can.

CLOCKS

(rest elbows on hips; extend forearms and index fingers up
    and move arms sideways slowly and rhythmically)
Big clocks make a sound like
Tick, Tock, Tick, Tock.
    (speak slowly)
Small clocks make a sound like
    (move arms faster)
Tick, tock, tick, tock.
And the very tiny clocks make a sound
    (move still faster)
Like tick, tick, tock, tock.
Tick, tock, tick, tock, tick, tock.

FIVE LITTLE PUMPKINS

(hold up five fingers and bend them down one
    at a time as verse progresses)
Five little pumpkins sitting on a gate;
The first one said, "My it's getting late."
The second one said, "There are witches in the air."
The third one said, "But we don't care."
The fourth one said, "Let's run, let's run."
The fifth one said, "It's Halloween fun."
"Wooooooo" went the wind,
    (sway hand through the air)
And out went the lights.
    (loud clap)
These five little pumpkins ran fast out of sight.
    (place hands behind back)

FRIENDS

I like my friends,
So when we are at play,
I try to be very kind
And nice in every way.

GOBBLE, GOBBLE

A turkey is a funny bird,
His head goes wobble, wobble.
    (place hands together and move back and forth)
And he knows just one word,
Gobble, gobble, gobble.

GRANDMA'S SPECTACLES

(bring index finger and thumb together and place against face
    as if wearing glasses)
These are Grandma's spectacles.
This is Grandma's hat.
    (bring fingertips together in a peak over head)
This is the way she folds her hands,
    (clasp hands together)
And lays them in her lap.
    (lay hands in lap)

HERE IS A BALL

Here is a ball,
    (touch fingers of both hands to form a ball)
Here is a bigger ball,
    (bow the arms with fingers touching to form a second ball)
And here is the biggest ball of all.
    (extend arms and do not touch fingers)
Now let us count the balls we made:
    One,
    Two,
    Three
    (repeat making the balls to reinforce the concepts by
    showing the increasing size)

HICKORY, DICKORY, DOCK

Hickory, dickory, dock.
The mouse ran up the clock.
The clock struck one, the mouse ran down,
Hickory, dickory, dock.

I LOOKED INSIDE MY MIRROR

I looked inside my mirror
To see what I could see.
It looks like I am happy today,
Because that smiling face is me.

I LOVE MY FAMILY

Some families are large.
    (spread arms out wide)
Some families are small.
    (bring arms close together)
But I love my family
    (cross arms over chest)
Best of all!

JACK AND JILL

Jack and Jill went up a hill
To fetch a pail of water.
Jack fell down and broke his crown
And Jill fell tumbling after.

JACK-IN-THE-BOX

Jack-in-the-box
Sit so still
    (squat or stoop down, placing hands over head as a cover)
Won't you come out?
Yes, I will!
    (open hands and jump up)

LITTLE JACK HORNER

Little Jack Horner
Sat in a corner
Eating a Christmas pie.
   (*pretend you're eating*)
He put in his thumb,
   (*point thumb down*)
And pulled out a plum
   (*point thumb up*)
And said, "What a good boy am I!"
   (*say out loud*)

LITTLE MISS MUFFET

Little Miss Muffet
Sat on a tuffet
Eating her curds and whey.
Along came a spider
And sat down beside her
And frightened Miss Muffet away!

RING AROUND THE ROSIE

(*teacher and children hold hands and walk around
   in a circle*)
Ring around the rosie,
A pocket full of posies,
Ashes, ashes,
We all fall down.
   (*everyone falls to the ground*)

THE MONKEY

The monkey claps, claps, claps his hands.
   (*clap hands*)
The monkey claps, claps his hands.
   (*clap hands*)
Monkey see, monkey do,
The monkey does the same as you.
   (*use pointer finger*)

The monkey pats his arm, pats his arm.
   (*pat arm*)
The monkey pats his arm, pats his arm.
   (*pat arm*)
Monkey see, monkey do,
The monkey does the same as you.
   (*use pointer finger*)

The monkey touches his head, touches his head.
   (*touch head*)
The monkey touches his head, touches his head.
   (*touch head*)
Monkey see, monkey do,
The monkey does the same as you.
   (*use pointer finger*)

The monkey gives a big smile, gives a big smile.
   (*smile big*)
The monkey gives a big smile, gives a big smile.
   (*smile big*)

Monkey see, monkey do,
The monkey does the same as you.
   (*use pointer finger*)

The monkey crawls all around, crawls all around.
   (*get down on hands and knees and crawl*)
The monkey crawls all around, crawls all around.
   (*get down on hands and knees and crawl*)
Monkey see, monkey do,
The monkey does the same as you.
   (*use pointer finger*)

THE MUFFIN MAN

Oh, do you know the muffin man,
The muffin man, the muffin man?
Oh, do you know the muffin man
Who lives on Drury Lane?
Yes, I know the muffin man,
The muffin man, the muffin man.
Oh, yes, I know the muffin man
Who lives on Drury Lane.

THE MULBERRY BUSH

(*Since this is a lengthy finger play, begin with just a verse or
two and then gradually individually add the remaining verses
as the toddlers gain proficiency.*)

Here we go 'round the mulberry bush,
The mulberry bush, the mulberry bush.
Here we go 'round the mulberry bush,
So early in the morning.

This is the way we wash our clothes,
Wash our clothes, wash our clothes.
This is the way we wash our clothes,
So early Monday morning.

This is the way we iron our clothes,
Iron our clothes, iron our clothes.
This is the way we iron our clothes,
So early Tuesday morning.

This is the way we scrub our clothes,
Scrub our clothes, scrub our clothes.
This is the way we scrub our clothes,
So early Wednesday morning.

This is the way we mend our clothes,
Mend our clothes, mend our clothes.
This is the way we mend our clothes,
So early Thursday morning.

This is the way we sweep the house,
Sweep the house, sweep the house.
This is the way we sweep the house,
So early Friday morning.

This is the way we bake our bread,
Bake our bread, bake our bread.
This is the way we bake our bread,
So early Saturday morning.

This is the way we go to church,
Go to church, go to church.
This is the way we go to church,
So early Sunday morning.

(The children can join hands with you and skip around in a circle. They can act out the words of the song beginning with the second verse. If church is inappropriate for Sunday, another activity can be substituted such as barbeque, play ball, mow the lawn, etc.)

MY PUPPY

I like to pet my puppy.
   (pet puppy)
He has such nice soft fur.
   (pet puppy)
And if I don't pull his tail
   (pull tail)
He won't say, "Grr!"
   (make face)

MY RABBIT

My rabbit has two big ears
   (hold up index and middle fingers for ears)
And a funny little nose.
   (join the other fingers for a nose)
He likes to nibble carrots
   (separate thumb from other two fingers)
And he hops wherever he goes.
   (move whole hand jerkily)

MY TOOTHBRUSH

I have a little toothbrush.
   (use pointer finger)
I hold it very tight.
   (make hand into fist.)
I brush my teeth each morning,
And then again at night.
   (use pointer finger and pretend to brush)

MY TURTLE

This is my turtle.
   (make fist; extend thumb)
He lives in a shell.
   (hide thumb in fist)
He likes his home very well.
He pokes his head out when he wants to eat.
   (extend thumb)
And pulls it back when he wants to sleep.
   (hide thumb in fist)

OLD KING COLE

Old King Cole was a merry old soul
   (lift elbows up and down)
And a merry old soul was he.
   (nod head)

He called for his pipe.
   (clap two times)
He called for his bowl.
   (clap two times)
And he called for his fiddlers three.
   (clap two times then pretend to play violin)

ONE, TWO, BUCKLE MY SHOE

One, two, buckle my shoe.
   (count on fingers as verse progresses)
Three, four, shut the door.
   (suit actions to words)
Five, six, pick up sticks.
Seven, eight, lay them straight.
Nine, ten, a big tall hen.

OPEN, SHUT THEM

Open, shut them.
   (suit actions to words)
Open, shut them.
Open, shut them.
Give a little clap.
Open, shut them.
Open, shut them.
Put them in your lap.
Creep them, creep them
Right up to your chin.
Open up your little mouth,
But do not put them in.
Open, shut them.
Open, shut them.
Open, shut them.
To your shoulders fly,
Then like little birdies
Let them flutter to the sky.
Falling, falling almost to the ground,
Quickly pick them up again and turn
Them round and round.
Faster, faster, faster.
Slower, slower, slower.
   (repeat first verse)

PAT-A-CAKE

Pat-a-cake, pat-a-cake, baker's man.
Bake me a cake as fast as you can!
   (clap hands together lightly)
Roll it
   (roll hands)
And pat it
   (touch hands together lightly)
And mark it with a *B*
   (write B in the air)
And put it in the oven for baby and me.
   (point to baby and yourself)

POPCORN CHANT 1

Popcorn, popcorn
Hot, hot, hot
Popcorn, popcorn
Pop, pop, pop.

POPCORN CHANT 2

Popcorn, popcorn
In a pot
What'll happen when you get hot?
Boom! Pop. Boom! Pop. Pop.
That's what happens when you get hot!

POPCORN CHANT 3

Popcorn, popcorn
In a dish
How many pieces do you wish?
1, 2, 3, 4
Eat those up and have some more!

RAINDROPS

Rain is falling down.
Rain is falling down.
    (*raise arm, flutter fingers to the ground, tapping the floor*)
Pitter-patter
Pitter-patter
Rain is falling down.

READY NOW, LET'S GO

I am a little kitty,
I have to tippy toe.
Come and do it with me.
Ready now, let's go.
    (*take tiny steps*)

I am a little rabbit.
I love to hop, hop, hop.
Come and do it with me.
It's fun we will never stop.
    (*hop around*)

I am a big bird.
I love to fly around using my wings.
Come and do it with me.
Ready now? Let's go.
    (*use arms as wings to fly*)

I am a great big elephant.
I take big steps so slow.
I'd love to have you join me.
Ready now? Let's go
    (*take slow, big steps*)

I am a little puppy.
I love to run and run.
Come and do it with me.
We will have such fun.
    (*run like a puppy*)

RIGHT HAND, LEFT HAND

This is my right hand,
I'll raise it up high.
    (*raise the right hand up high*)
This is my left hand.
I'll touch the sky.
    (*raise the left hand up high*)
Right hand,
    (*show right palm*)
Left hand,
    (*show left palm*)
Roll them around
    (*roll hands over and over*)
Left hand,
    (*show palm*)
Right hand,
    (*show palm*)
Pound, pound, pound.
    (*hit fists together*)

SEE, SEE, SEE

See, see, see
    (*shade eyes with hands*)
Three birds are in a tree.
    (*hold up three fingers*)
One can chirp
    (*point to thumb*)
And one can sing
    (*point to index finger*)
One is just a tiny thing.
    (*point to middle finger, then rock baby bird in arms*)
See, see, see
Three birds are in a tree.
    (*hold up three fingers*)

STAND UP TALL

Stand up tall
Hands in the air.
Now sit down
In your chair.
Clap your hands
And make a frown.
Smile and smile.
Hop like a clown.

TEAPOT

I'm a little teapot,
   (*place right hand on hip, extend left, palm out*)
Short and stout.
Here's my handle.
And here's my spout.
When I get all steamed up, I just shout:
"Tip me over, and pour me out."
   (*bend to left*)
I can change my handle
   (*place left hand on hip and extend right hand out*)
And my spout.
"Tip me over, and pour me out."
   (*bend to the right*)

TEDDY BEAR

Teddy bear, teddy bear, turn around.
Teddy bear, teddy bear, touch the ground.
Teddy bear, teddy bear, climb the stairs.
Teddy bear, teddy bear, jump into bed.
Teddy bear, teddy bear, turn out the lights.
Teddy bear, teddy bear, blow a kiss.
Teddy bear, teddy bear, say goodnight.
Goodnight.

TEN LITTLE DUCKS

Ten little ducks swimming in the lake.
   (*move ten fingers as if swimming*)
Quack! Quack!
   (*snap fingers twice*)
They give their heads a shake.
   (*shake fingers*)
Glunk! Glunk! Go go little frogs.
   (*two claps of hands*)
And away to their mothers,
The ten ducks run.
   (*move hands in running motion from front to back*)

TEN LITTLE FINGERS

I have ten little fingers and ten little toes.
   (*children point to portions of body as they repeat words*)
Two little arms and one little nose.
One little mouth and two little ears.
Two little eyes for smiles and tears.
One little head and two little feet.
One little chin, that makes _____ complete.

THIS LITTLE PIGGY

This little piggy went to market.
   (*point to one finger at a time*)
This little piggy stayed home.
This little piggy had roast beef.
This little piggy had none.
This little piggy cried, "Wee, wee, wee."
And ran all the way home.

THREE FROGS

Three little frogs
   (*hold up three fingers of left hand*)
Asleep in the sun.
   (*fold them over*)
We'll creep up and wake them.
   (*make creeping motion with fingers of right hand*)
Then we will run.
   (*hold up three fingers while right hand runs away*)

THREE LITTLE DUCKIES

Three little duckies
   (*hold up three fingers*)
Swimming in the lake.
   (*make swimming motions*)
The first ducky said,
   (*hold up one finger*)
"Watch the waves I make."
   (*make wave motions*)
The second ducky said,
   (*hold up two fingers*)
"Swimming is such fun."
   (*smile*)
The third ducky said,
   (*hold up three fingers*)
"I'd rather sit in the sun."
   (*turn face to sun*)
Then along came a motorboat.
With a Pop! Pop! Pop!
   (*clap three times*)
And three little duckies
Swam away from the spot.
   (*put three fingers behind back*)

THREE LITTLE MONKEYS

Three little monkeys jumping on the bed.
   (*hold up three fingers*)
One fell off and bumped his head.
Mama called the doctor and the doctor said,
No more monkeys jumping on the bed.
   (*shake pointer finger as if scolding*)

Two little monkeys jumping on the bed,
   (*hold up two fingers*)
One fell off and bumped his head.
Mama called the doctor and the doctor said,
No more monkeys jumping on the bed.
   (*shake pointer finger as if scolding*)

One little monkey jumping on the bed.
   (*hold up one finger*)
He fell off and bumped his head.
Mama called the doctor and the doctor said,
No more jumping on the bed.
   (*shake pointer finger as if scolding*)

TWO LITTLE APPLES

(*hold hands above head, form circles with thumb
and forefinger of each hand*)
Away up high in the apple tree,
Two red apples smiled at me.
(*smile*)
I shook that tree as hard as I could.
(*put hands out as if on tree—shake*)
And down they came.
(*hands above head and lower to ground*)
And ummmmm were they good!
(*rub tummy*)

TWO LITTLE BLACKBIRDS

Two little blackbirds sitting on a hill.
(*show two fingers*)
One named Jack.
(*hold up one finger on right hand*)
One named Jill.
(*hold up one finger on the left hand*)
Fly away Jack.
(*move right hand behind back*)
Fly away Jill.
(*move the left hand behind back*)
Come back Jack.
(*return right hand*)
Come back Jill.
(*return left hand*)
(Children's names can be substituted for Jack and Jill in
this finger play.)

TWO LITTLE KITTENS

(*hold up two fingers, cup hands together to form a ball*)
Two little kittens found a ball of yarn
As they were playing near a barn.
(*bring hands together pointed upward for barn*)
One little kitten jumped in the hay,
(*hold up one finger, make jumping then wiggling motion*)
The other little kitten ran away.
(*make running motion with other hand*)

ZOO ANIMALS

This is the way the elephant goes.
(*clasp hands together, extend arms, move back and forth*)
With a curly trunk instead of a nose.
The buffalo, all shaggy and fat.
Has two sharp horns in place of a hat.
(*point to forehead*)
The hippo with his mouth so wide
Let's see what's inside.
(*hands together and open wide and close them*)
The wiggly snake upon the ground
Crawls along without a sound.
(*weave hands back and forth*)
But monkey see and monkey do is the
funniest animal in the zoo.
(*place thumbs in ears and wiggle fingers*)

Songs

Music is a universal language and a natural form of expression for children of all ages. Infants need to have a wide variety of music experiences that are casual and spontaneous. They enjoy lullabies that are slow, soft, and soothing. In addition to lullabies, classical, folk and music from different ethnic and cultural groups should all be included. Children like songs about animals and familiar objects, which tell a story and contain frequent repetition. Choose simple songs with a strong melody that represent their age, abilities, and interests. Chances are children will more easily remember these songs. While singing, remember to convey enthusiasm.

Music is a valuable experience for young children. They enjoy listening to music while engaged in activities and napping. Music promotes the development of listening skills and builds vocabulary. It is a tool that provides an opportunity for learning new concepts such as up/down, fast/slow, heavy/light, and loud/soft. Music releases tension, stimulates the imagination, and promotes the development of auditory memory skills.

ALL ABOUT ME

Brushing Teeth
(Tune: "Mulberry Bush")
This is the way we brush our teeth,
Brush our teeth, brush our teeth.
This is the way we brush our teeth,
So early in the morning.

Good Morning
Good morning to you.
Good morning to you.
We're all in our places,
With bright shining faces,
Good morning to you.

ANIMALS

The Animals on the Farm
(Tune: "The Wheels on the Bus")
The cows on the farm go moo, moo, moo,
Moo, moo, moo, moo, moo, moo.
The cows on the farm go moo, moo, moo,
All day long.

The horses on the farm go nay, nay, nay,
Nay, nay, nay, nay, nay, nay.
The horses on the farm go nay, nay, nay,
All day long.

OTHER VERSES:
Pigs—oink
Sheep—baa
Chicken—cluck
Turkeys—gobble

The Ants Go Marching One by One
The ants go marching one by one.
Hurrah! Hurrah!
The ants go marching one by one.
Hurrah! Hurrah!
The ants go marching one by one.

The little one stops to suck her thumb
And they all go marching,
Down in the ground
To get out of the rain.
Boom Boom Boom

OTHER VERSES:
Two by two
The little one stops to tie his shoe
Three by three
The little one stops to scratch her knee
Four by four
The little one stops to shut the door
Five by five
The little one stops to wave goodbye.

Circus
(Tune: "Did You Ever See a Lassie")
Let's pretend that we are clowns, are clowns, are clowns.
Let's pretend that we are clowns.
We'll have so much fun.
We'll put on our makeup and make people laugh hard.
Let's pretend that we are clowns.
We'll have so much fun.

Let's pretend that we are elephants, are elephants, are elephants.
Let's pretend that we are elephants.
We'll have so much fun.
We'll sway back and forth and stand on just two legs.
Let's pretend that we are elephants.
We'll have so much fun.

Let's pretend that we are on a trapeze, a trapeze, a trapeze.
Let's pretend that we are on a trapeze.
We'll have so much fun.
We'll swing high and swoop low and make people shout "oh"!
Let's pretend that we are on a trapeze.
We'll have so much fun!

Easter Bunny
(Tune: "Ten Little Indians")
Where, oh, where is the Easter Bunny,
Where, oh, where is the Easter Bunny,
Where, oh, where is the Easter Bunny,
Early Easter morning?

Find all the eggs and put them in a basket,
Find all the eggs and put them in a basket,
Find all the eggs and put them in a basket,
Early Easter morning.

Itsy Bitsy Spider
The itsy bitsy spider went up the water spout
Down came the rain and washed the spider out
Out came the sun and dried up all the rain
And the itsy bitsy spider went up the spout again.
(This is also a popular finger play.)

Kitty
(Tune: "Bingo")
I have a cat. She's very shy.
But she comes when I call Kitty
K-I-T-T-Y
K-I-T-T-Y
K-I-T-T-Y
and Kitty is her name-o.

(Variation: Let children think of other names.)

Old MacDonald Had a Farm
Old MacDonald had a farm,
E-I-E-I-O.
And on his farm he had some cows,
E-I-E-I-O.
With a moo, moo here and a moo, moo there,
Here a moo, there a moo, everywhere a moo, moo.
Old MacDonald had a farm,
E-I-E-I-O.

OTHER VERSES:
Sheep—baa, baa
Pigs—oink, oink
Ducks—quack, quack
Chickens—chick, chick

Two Little Black Bears
(Tune: "Two Little Blackbirds")
Two little black bears sitting on a hill
One named Jack, one named Jill.
Run away Jack
Run away Jill.
Come back Jack
Come back Jill.
Two little black bears sitting on a hill
One named Jack, one named Jill.

CLEANUP SONGS

Cleanup Time 1
(Tune: "London Bridge")
Cleanup time is already here,
Already here, already here.
Cleanup time is already here,
Already here.

Cleanup Time 2
(Tune: "Hot Cross Buns")
Cleanup time.
Cleanup time.
Put all of the toys away.
It's cleanup time.

Do You Know What Time It Is?
(Tune: "The Muffin Man")
Oh, do you know what time it is,
What time it is, what time it is?
Oh, do you know what time it is?
It's almost cleanup time.
  (Or, it's time to clean up.)

A Helper I Will Be
(Tune: "The Farmer in the Dell")
A helper I will be.
A helper I will be.
I'll pick up the toys and put them away.
A helper I will be.

It's Cleanup Time
(Tune: "Looby Loo")
It's cleanup time at the preschool.
It's time for boys and girls
To stop what they are doing.
And put away their toys.

Oh, It's Cleanup Time
(Tune: "Oh, My Darling Clementine")
Oh, it's cleanup time,
Oh, it's cleanup time,
Oh, it's cleanup time right now.
It's time to put the toys away,
It is cleanup time right now.

Passing Around
(Tune: "Skip to My Loo")
Brad, take a napkin and pass them to Sara.
Sara, take a napkin and pass them to Tina.
Tina, take a napkin and pass them to Eric.
Passing around the napkins.

(Fill in the appropriate child's name and substitute for "napkin" any object that needs to be passed at mealtime.)

Put Your Coat On
(Tune: "Oh, My Darling Clementine")
Put your coat on.
Put your coat on.
Put your winter coat on now.
We are going to play outside.
Put your coat on right now.
(Change "coat" to any article of clothing.)

This Is the Way
(Tune: "Mulberry Bush")
This is the way we pick up our toys,
Pick up our toys, pick up our toys.
This is the way we pick up our toys,
At cleanup time each day.
*(Substituting "before bedtime" opposed to "cleanup time"
could modify this song.)*

Time to Clean up
(Tune: "Are You Sleeping?")
Time to clean up.
Time to clean up.
Everybody help.
Everybody help.
Put the toys away, put the toys away.
Then sit down. (Or, then come here.)
(Specific toys can be mentioned in place of "toys.")

We're Cleaning Up Our Room
(Tune: "The Farmer in the Dell")
We're cleaning up our room.
We're cleaning up our room.
We're putting all the toys away.
We're cleaning up our room.

FAVORITES

London Bridge
London Bridge is falling down,
Falling down, falling down.
London Bridge is falling down.
My fair lady.

Twinkle, Twinkle, Little Star
Twinkle, twinkle, little star,
How I wonder what you are!
Up above the world so high,
Like a diamond in the sky.
Twinkle, twinkle, little star,
How I wonder what you are!

Where Is Thumbkin?
Where is thumbkin?
Where is thumbkin?
Here I am,
Here I am.
How are you today, sir?
Very well, I thank you.
Fly away, fly away.

OTHER VERSES:
Pointer
Tall man
Ring man
Pinky

FEELINGS

Feelings
(Tune: "Twinkle, Twinkle, Little Star")
I have feelings.
You do, too.
Let's all sing about a few.
I am happy. *(smile)*
I am sad. *(frown)*
I get scared. *(wrap arms around self)*
I get mad. *(sneer and wrinkle nose)*
I am proud of being me. *(hands on hips)*
That's a feeling, too, you see.
I have feelings. *(point to self)*
You do, too. *(point to someone else)*
We just sang about a few.

If You're Happy and You Know It
If you're happy and you know it
Clap your hands.
   (clap twice)
If you're happy and you know it
Clap your hands.
   (clap twice)
If you're happy and you know it
Then your face will surely show it.
If you're happy and you know it
Clap your hands.
   (clap twice)

If you're sad and you know it
Say boo-hoo.
   (rub your eyes)
If you're sad and you know it
Say boo-hoo.
   (rub your eyes)
If you're sad and you know it
Then your face will surely show it.
If you're sad and you know it
Say boo-hoo.
   (rub your eyes)

If you're mad and you know it
Wrinkle your nose.
   (wrinkle nose)
If you're mad and you know it
Wrinkle your nose.
   (wrinkle nose)
If you're mad and you know it
Then your face will surely show it.
If you're mad and you know it
Wrinkle your nose.
   (wrinkle nose)

PEOPLE

Are You Sleeping?
Are you sleeping?
Are you sleeping?
Brother John, brother John,
Morning bells are ringing,
Morning bells are ringing.
Ding, ding, dong!
Ding, ding, dong!

Do You Know This Friend of Mine?
(Tune: "The Muffin Man")
Do you know this friend of mine,
This friend of mine,
This friend of mine?
Do you know this friend of mine?
Her name is _____.
Yes, we know this friend of yours,
This friend of yours,
This friend of yours.
Yes, we know this friend of yours.
Her name is _____.

The Muffin Man
Oh, do you know the muffin man,
The muffin man, the muffin man?
Oh, do you know the muffin man,
Who lives on Drury Lane?

Oh, yes we know the muffin man,
The muffin man, the muffin man.
Oh, yes we know the muffin man,
Who lives on Drury Lane.

Oh, how do you know the muffin man,
The muffin man, the muffin man?
Oh, how do you know the muffin man,
Who lives on Drury Lane.

Cause [Papaw] is the muffin man,
The muffin man, the muffin man.
[Pawpaw] is the muffin man,
Who lives on Drury Lane.

(Substitute names of other males who are important in the child's life, such as Daddy or Uncle Todd.)

This Old Man
This old man
He played one
He played knick knack on a drum
With a knick knack, paddy whack
Give the dog a bone
This old man came rolling home.

OTHER VERSES:
He played two
He played knick knack on my shoe.
He played three
He played knick knack on a tree
He played four
He played knick knack at my door
He played five
He played knick knack on a hive.

TRANSPORTATION

Row, Row, Row, Your Boat
Row, row, row your boat.
Gently down the stream.
Merrily, merrily, merrily, merrily,
Life is but a dream.

The Wheels on the Bus
The wheels on the bus go round and round.
Round and round, round and round.
The wheels on the bus go round and round.
All around the town.

OTHER VERSES:
The wipers on the bus go swish, swish, swish.
The doors on the bus go open and shut.
The horn on the bus goes beep, beep, beep.
The driver on the bus says, "Move on back."
The people on the bus go up and down.

Rhythm Instruments

Using rhythm instruments is a method of teaching young children to express themselves. Rhythm instruments can be common household objects or purchased through school supply stores or catalogs. Examples include:

Commercially Purchased	Household Items
Drums	Pots
Jingle sticks	Pans
Cymbals	Lids
Rattles	Wooden spoons
Wrist bells	Aluminum pie pans
Shakers	Metal whisks
Maracas	Plastic bowls
Sandpaper blocks	

You can also improvise and construct these instruments—save cans, cardboard tubes that have plastic lids from nuts, chips, and coffee. These items can be used as drums. If you place noise-making objects inside the cans or tubes, they can be used as shakers. However, make sure that you secure the lid using a high-quality adhesive tape that children cannot remove.

Resources Related to Infants

The authors and Delmar make every effort to ensure that all Internet resources are accurate at the time of printing. However, due to the fluid, time-sensitive nature of the Internet, we cannot guarantee that all URLs and Web site addresses will remain current for the duration of this edition.

The American Montessori Society Bulletin
American Montessori Society (AMS)
281 Park Avenue South, 6th Floor
New York, NY 10010-6102
(212) 358-1250; (212) 358-1256 FAX
www.amshq.org

Babybug
Cricket Magazine Group
PO Box 7437
Red Oak, IA 51591-2437
(800) 827-0227
www.babybugmag.com

The Black Child Advocate
National Black Child Development Institute
(NBCDI)
1101 15th Street NW, Suite 900
Washington, DC 20005
(202) 833-2220; (202) 833-8222 FAX
www.nbcdi.org

Child and Youth Quarterly
Human Sciences Press
233 Spring Street, Floor 5
New York, NY 10013-1522
(212) 620-8000

*Child Development and Child Development Abstracts
and Bibliography*
Society for Research in Child Development
University of Michigan
505 East Huron, Suite 301
Ann Arbor, MI 48104-1567
(734) 998-6578; (734) 998-6569 FAX
www.srcd.org

Child Health Alert
PO Box 610228
Newton Highlands, MA 02161
(781) 239-1762
ericps.ed.uiuc.edu/npin/nls/chalert.html

*Childhood Education; Journal of Research in Early
Childhood Education*
Association for Childhood Education
International (ACEI)
17904 Georgia Avenue; Suite 215
Olney, MD 20832
(301) 570-2111; (301) 570-2212 FAX
www.udel.edu/bateman/acei

Child Welfare
Child Welfare League of America (CWLA)
440 First Street NW, 3rd Floor
Washington, DC 20001-2085
(202) 638-2952; (202) 638-4004 FAX
www.cwla.org

Children Today
Superintendent of Documents
U.S. Government Printing Office
Washington, DC 20402
www.access.gpo.gov

Early Childhood Education Journal
Human Sciences Press
233 Spring Street, Floor 5
New York, NY 10013-1522
(212) 620-8000
www.wkap.nl/journalhome.htm/1082-3301

Developmental Psychology
American Psychological Association
750 First Street NE
Washington, DC 20002-4242
(202) 336-5500
www.apa.org

Dimensions of Early Childhood
Southern Association for Children Under Six
Box 56130 Brady Station
Little Rock, AR 72215
(800) 305-7322; (501) 227-5297 FAX

Early Child Development and Care
Gordon and Breach Publishing
Box 32160
Newark, NJ 07102
(800) 545-8398
www.gbhap.com

Earlychildhood NEWS
Earlychildhood.com
2 Lower Ragsdale, Suite 125
Monterey, CA 93940
(831) 333-5501; (800) 627-2829;
(831) 333-5510 FAX
www.earlychildhood.com

Early Childhood Research Quarterly
National Association for the Education of Young
Children (NAEYC)
1509 16th Street NW
Washington, DC 20036-1426
(202) 232-8777; (202) 328-1846 FAX
www.naeyc.org

Educational Leadership
Association for Supervision and Curriculum
Development (ASCD)
1703 North Beauregard Street
Alexandria, VA 22311-1714
(703) 578-9600; (800) 933-ASCD;
(703) 575-5400 FAX
www.ascd.org

Educational Researcher
American Educational Research Association
(AERA)
1230 17th Street NW
Washington, DC 20036
(202) 223-9485; (202) 775-1824 FAX
www.aera.net

ERIC/EECE
University of Illinois
Children's Research Center
51 Gerty Drive
Champaign, IL 61820-7469
http://ericps.ed.uiuc.edu/eece

Exceptional Children
Council for Exceptional Children
1110 North Glebe Road, Suite 300
Arlington, VA 22201-5704
(703) 620-3660; (888) CEC-SPED;
(703) 264-9494 FAX
www.cec.sped.org

Gifted Child Quarterly
National Association for Gifted Children
1707 L Street NW, Suite 550
Washington, DC 20036
(202) 785-4268
www.nagc.org

Instructor
Scholastic, Inc.
555 Broadway
New York, NY 10012
www.scholastic.com/instructor

Journal of Family and Consumer Sciences
American Association of Family and Consumer
Services (AAFCS)
1555 King Street
Alexandria, VA 22314
(703) 706-4600; (703) 706-4663 FAX
www.aafcs.org

Young Children
National Association for the Education of Young
Children (NAEYC)
1509 16th Street NW
Washington, DC 20036-1426
(202) 232-8777; (202) 328-1846 FAX
www.naeyc.org

Other information may be obtained through various
professional organizations.

The following groups may be able to provide you with
other resources:

American Association for Gifted Children
Box 90270
Durham, NC 27708-0270
www.aagc.org

*American Association of Family and Consumer Services
(AAFCS)*
1555 King Street
Alexandria, VA 22314
(703) 706-4600; (703) 706-4663 FAX
www.aafcs.org

American Montessori Association (AMS)
281 Park Avenue South, 6th Floor
New York, NY 10010
(212) 358-1250; (212) 358-1256 FAX
www.amshq.org

*Association for Childhood Education International
(ACEI)*
17904 Georgia Avenue, Suite 215
Olney, MD 20832
(301) 570-2111; (800) 423-3563;
(301) 570-2212 FAX
www.udel.edu/bateman/acei

Association for Supervision and Curriculum
Development (ASCD)
1703 North Beauregard Street
Alexandria, VA 22311-1714
(703) 578-9600; (800) 933-ASCD;
(703) 575-5400 FAX
www.ascd.org

Canadian Association for the Education of Young
Children (CAYC)
612 West 23rd Street
Vancouver, BC V7M 2C3
www.cayc.ca

Children's Defense Fund
25 E Street NW
Washington, DC 20001
(202) 628-8787
www.childrensdefense.org

Child Welfare League of America
440 First Street NW, 3rd Floor
Washington, DC 20001-2085
(202) 638-2952; (202) 638-4004 FAX
www.cwla.org

Council for Exceptional Children
1110 North Glebe Road, Suite 300
Arlington, VA 22201-5704
(703) 620-3660; (888) CEC-SPED;
(703) 264-9494 FAX
www.cec.sped.org

International Reading Association
800 Barksdale Road
PO Box 8139
Newark, DE 19714-8139
(302) 731-1600; (302) 731-1057 FAX
www.reading.org

National Association for the Education of Young
Children (NAEYC)
1509 16th Street NW
Washington, DC 20036-1426
(202) 232-8777; (202) 328-1846 FAX
www.naeyc.org

National Association for Gifted Children
1707 L Street NW, Suite 550
Washington, DC 20036
(202) 785-4268
www.nagc.org

National Black Child Development Institute (NBCDI)
1101 15th Street NW, Suite 900
Washington, DC 20005
(202) 833-2220; (202) 833-8222 FAX
www.nbcdi.org

National Committee to Prevent Child Abuse
2950 Tennyson Street
Denver, CO 80212
(303) 433-2451; (303) 433-9701 FAX
www.childabuse.org

National Education Association (NEA)
1201 16th Street NW
Washington, DC 20036
(202) 833-4000
www.nea.org

Society for Research in Child Development
University of Michigan
505 East Huron, Suite 301
Ann Arbor, MI 48104-1567
(734) 998-6578; (734) 998-6569 FAX
www.srcd.org

Developmental Checklist

Child's Name: _____

Observer's Name: _____

Observation Date: _____

PHYSICAL DEVELOPMENT	OBSERVED	
Birth to Three Months	Date	Comments
Acts reflexively—sucking, stepping, rooting		
Swipes at objects in front of body, uncoordinated		
Holds head erect and steady when lying on stomach		
Lifts head and shoulders		
Rolls from side to back		
Follows moving objects with eyes		
Four to Six Months		
Holds cube in hand		
Reaches for objects with one hand		
Rolls from back to side		
Reaches for objects in front of body, coordinated		
Sits with support		
Transfers objects from hand to hand		
Grabs objects with either hand		
Sits in tripod position using arms for support		
Seven to Nine Months		
Sits independently		
Stepping reflex returns, so that child bounces when held on a surface in a standing position		
Leans over and reaches when in a sitting position		
Gets on hands and knees but may fall forward		
Crawls		
Pulls to standing position		
Claps hands together		
Stands with adult's assistance		
Learns pincer grasp, using thumb with forefinger to pick up objects		
Uses finger and thumb to pick up objects		
Brings objects together with banging noises		

The developmental milestones listed are based on universal patterns of when various traits emerge. Because each child is unique certain traits may develop at an earlier or later age.

PHYSICAL DEVELOPMENT	OBSERVED	
Ten to Twelve Months	**Date**	**Comments**
Supports entire body weight on legs		
Walks when hands are held		
Cruises along furniture or steady objects		
Stands independently		
Walks independently		
Crawls up stairs or steps		
Voluntarily releases objects held in hands		
Has good balance when sitting; can shift positions without falling		
Takes off shoes and socks		
Thirteen to Eighteen Months		
Builds tower of two cubes		
Turns the pages of a cardboard book two or three at a time		
Scribbles vigorously		
Walks proficiently		
Walks while carrying or pulling a toy		
Walks up stairs with assistance		
Nineteen to Twenty-Four Months		
Walks up stairs independently, one step at a time		
Jumps in place		
Kicks a ball		
Runs in a modified fashion		
Shows a decided preference for one hand		
Completes a three-piece puzzle with knobs		
Builds a tower of six cubes		
Twenty-Five to Thirty-Six Months		
Maneuvers around obstacles in a pathway		
Runs in a more adult-like fashion; knees are slightly bent, arms move in the opposite direction		
Walks down stairs independently		
Marches to music		
Uses feet to propel wheeled riding toys		
Rides a tricycle		
Usually uses whole arm movements to paint or color		
Throws a ball forward, where intended		
Builds tower using eight or more blocks		
Imitates drawing circles and vertical and horizontal lines		
Turns pages in book one by one		
Fingers work together to scoop up small objects		
Strings large beads on a shoelace		

Additional Observations for Physical Development

The developmental milestones listed are based on universal patterns of when various traits emerge. Because each child is unique certain traits may develop at an earlier or later age.

LANGUAGE AND COMMUNICATION DEVELOPMENT	OBSERVED	
Birth to Three Months	Date	Comments
Communicates with cries, grunts, and facial expressions		
Prefers human voices		
Coos		
Laughs		
Smiles and coos to initiate and sustain interactions with caregiver		
Four to Six Months		
Babbles spontaneously		
Acquires sounds of native language in babble		
Canonical, systematic consonant-vowel pairings; babbling occurs		
Participates in interactive games initiated by adults		
Takes turns while interacting		
Seven to Nine Months		
Varies babble in loudness, pitch, and rhythm		
Adds *d, t, n,* and *w* to repertoire of babbling sounds		
Produces gestures to communicate often by pointing		
May say *mama* or *dada* but does not connect words with parents		
Ten to Twelve Months		
Uses preverbal gestures to influence the behavior of others		
Demonstrates word comprehension skills		
Waves good-bye		
Speaks recognizable first word		
Initiates familiar games with adults		
Thirteen to Eighteen Months		
Has expressive vocabulary of 10 to 20 words		
Engages in "jargon talk"		
Engages in telegraphic speech by combining two words together		
Experiences a burst of language development		
Comprehends approximately 50 words		
Nineteen to Twenty-Four Months		
Continues using telegraphic speech		
Able to combine three words		
Talks, 25 percent of words being understandable		
Refers to self by name		

The developmental milestones listed are based on universal patterns of when various traits emerge. Because each child is unique certain traits may develop at an earlier or later age.

LANGUAGE AND COMMUNICATION DEVELOPMENT	OBSERVED	
Nineteen to Twenty-Four Months (continued)	Date	Comments
Joins three or four words into a sentence		
Comprehends approximately 300 words		
Expressive language includes a vocabulary of approximately 250 words		
Twenty-Five to Thirty-Six Months		
Continues using telegraphic speech combining three or four words		
Speaks in complete sentences following word order of native language		
Displays effective conversational skills		
Refers to self as *me* or *I* rather than by name		
Talks about objects and events not immediately present		
Uses grammatical markers and some plurals		
Vocabulary increases rapidly, up to 300 words		
Enjoys being read to if allowed to participate by pointing, talking, and turning pages		

Additional Observations for Language and Communication Development

COGNITIVE DEVELOPMENT	OBSERVED	
Birth to Three Months	Date	Comments
Cries for assistance		
Acts reflexively		
Prefers to look at patterned objects, bull's-eye, horizontal stripes, and the human face		
Imitates adults' facial expressions		
Searches with eyes for sources of sounds		
Begins to recognize familiar people at a distance		
Discovers and repeats bodily actions such as sucking, swiping, and grasping		
Discovers hands and feet as extension of self		

The developmental milestones listed are based on universal patterns of when various traits emerge. Because each child is unique certain traits may develop at an earlier or later age.

COGNITIVE DEVELOPMENT (continued)		OBSERVED	
Four to Six Months	Date		Comments
Recognizes people by their voice			
Enjoys repeating acts, such as shaking a rattle, that produce results in the external world			
Searches with eyes for source of sounds			
Enjoys watching hands and feet			
Searches for a partially hidden object			
Uses toys in a purposeful manner			
Imitates simple actions			
Explores toys using existing schemas such as sucking, banging, grasping, shaking, etc.			
Seven to Nine Months			
Enjoys looking at books with familiar objects			
Distinguishes familiar from unfamiliar faces			
Engages in goal-directed behavior			
Anticipates events			
Finds objects that are totally hidden			
Imitates behaviors that are slightly different than those usually performed			
Begins to show interest in filling and dumping containers			
Ten to Twelve Months			
Solves sensorimotor problems by deliberately using schemas, such as shaking a container to empty its contents			
Points to body parts upon request			
Drops toys intentionally and repeatedly looks in the direction of the fallen object			
Waves good-bye			
Shows evidence of stronger memory capabilities			
Follows simple, one-step directions			
Categorizes objects by appearance			
Looks for objects hidden in a second location			
Thirteen to Eighteen Months			
Explores properties of objects by acting on them in novel ways			
Solves problems through trial and error			
Experiments with cause-and-effect relationships such as turning on televisions, banging on drums, etc.			
Plays body identification games			
Imitates novel behaviors of others			
Identifies family members in photographs			

The developmental milestones listed are based on universal patterns of when various traits emerge. Because each child is unique certain traits may develop at an earlier or later age.

COGNITIVE DEVELOPMENT	OBSERVED	
Nineteen to Twenty-Four Months	Date	Comments
Points to and identifies objects on request, such as when reading a book, touring, etc.		
Sorts by shapes and colors		
Recognizes self in photographs and mirror		
Demonstrates deferred imitation		
Engages in functional play		
Finds objects that have been moved while out of sight		
Solves problems with internal representation		
Categorizes self and others by gender, race, hair color, etc.		
Twenty-Five to Thirty-Six Months		
Uses objects for purposes other than intended		
Uses private speech while working		
Classifies objects based on one dimension, such as toy cars versus blocks		
Follows two-step directions		
Concentrates or attends to self-selected activities for longer periods of time		
Points to and labels objects spontaneously, such as when reading a book		
Coordinates pretend play with other children		
Gains a nominal sense of numbers through counting and labeling objects in a set		
Begins developing concepts about opposites such as big and small, tall and short, in and out		
Begins eveloping concepts about time such as today, tomorrow, and yesterday		

Additional Observations for Cognitive Development

The developmental milestones listed are based on universal patterns of when various traits emerge. Because each child is unique certain traits may develop at an earlier or later age.

SOCIAL DEVELOPMENT		OBSERVED
Birth to Three Months	Date	Comments
Turns head toward a speaking voice		
Recognizes primary caregiver		
Bonds to primary caregiver		
Finds comfort in the human face		
Displays a social smile		
Is quieted by a voice		
Begins to differentiate self from caregiver		
Four to Six Months		
Seeks out adults for play by crying, cooing, or smiling		
Responds with entire body to familiar face by looking at a person, smiling, kicking legs, and waving arms		
Participates actively in interactions with others by vocalizing in response to adult speech		
Smiles at familiar faces and stares solemnly at strangers		
Distinguishes between familiar and nonfamiliar adults and surroundings		
Seven to Nine Months		
Becomes upset when separated from a favorite adult		
Acts deliberately to maintain the presence of a favorite adult by clinging or crying		
Uses adults as a base for exploration, typically		
Looks to others who are exhibiting signs of distress		
Enjoys observing and interacting briefly with other children		
Likes to play and responds to games such as patty-cake and peekaboo		
Engages in solitary play		
Develops preferences for particular people and objects		
Shows distress when in the presence of a stranger		
Ten to Twelve Months		
Shows a decided preference for one or two caregivers		
Plays parallel to other children		
Enjoys playing with siblings		
Begins asserting self		
Begins developing a sense of humor		
Develops a sense of self-identity through the identification of body parts		
Begins distinguishing boys from girls		

The developmental milestones listed are based on universal patterns of when various traits emerge. Because each child is unique certain traits may develop at an earlier or later age.

SOCIAL DEVELOPMENT		OBSERVED
Thirteen to Eighteen Months	Date	Comments
Demands personal attention		
Imitates behaviors of others		
Becoming increasingly aware of the self as a separate being		
Shares affection with people other than primary caregiver		
Shows ownership of possessions		
Begins developing a view of self as autonomous when completing tasks independently		
Nineteen to Twenty-Four Months		
Shows enthusiasm for company of others		
Views the world only from own, egocentric perspective		
Plays contentedly alone or near adults		
Engages in functional play		
Defends possessions		
Recognizes self in photographs or mirrors		
Refers to self with pronouns such as *I* or *me*		
Categorizes people by using salient characteristics such as race or hair color		
Shows less fear of strangers		
Twenty-five to Thirty-Six Months		
Observes others to see how they do things		
Engages primarily in solitary or parallel play		
Sometimes offers toys to other children		
Begins to play cooperatively with other children		
Engages in sociodramatic play		
Wants to do things independently		
Asserts independence by using "no" a lot		
Develops a rudimentary awareness that others have wants or feelings that may be different than their own		
Makes demands of or "bosses" parents, guardians, and caregivers		
Uses physical aggression less and uses words to solve problems		
Engages in gender stereotypical behavior		

Additional Observations for Social Development

The developmental milestones listed are based on universal patterns of when various traits emerge. Because each child is unique certain traits may develop at an earlier or later age.

EMOTIONAL DEVELOPMENT		OBSERVED
Birth to Three Months	Date	Comments
Feels and expresses three basic emotions: interest, distress, and disgust		
Cries to signal a need		
Quiets in response to being held, typically		
Feels and expresses enjoyment		
Shares a social smile		
Reads and distinguishes adults' facial expressions		
Begins to self-regulate emotional expressions		
Laughs aloud		
Quiets self by using techniques such as sucking a thumb or pacifier		
Four to Six Months		
Expresses delight		
Responds to the emotions of caregivers		
Begins to distinguish familiar from unfamiliar people		
Shows a preference for being held by a familiar person		
Begins to assist with holding a bottle		
Expresses happiness selectively by laughing and smiling more with familiar people		
Seven to Nine Months		
Responds to social events by using the face, gaze, voice, and posture to form coherent emotional patterns		
Expresses fear and anger more often		
Begins to regulate emotions through moving into or out of experiences		
Begins to detect the meaning of others' emotional expressions		
Looks to others for clues on how to react		
Shows fear of strangers		
Ten to Twelve Months		
Continues to exhibit delight, happiness, discomfort, anger, and sadness		
Expresses anger when goals are blocked		
Expresses anger at the source of frustration		
Begins to show compliance to caregivers' requests		
Often objects to having playtime stopped		
Begins eating with a spoon		
Assists in dressing and undressing		
Acts in loving, caring ways toward dolls or stuffed animals, typically		
Feeds self a complete meal when served finger foods		
Claps when successfully completing a task		

The developmental milestones listed are based on universal patterns of when various traits emerge. Because each child is unique certain traits may develop at an earlier or later age.

EMOTIONAL DEVELOPMENT	OBSERVED	
Thirteen to Eighteen Months	Date	Comments
Exhibits autonomy by frequently saying "no"		
Labels several emotions		
Connects feelings with social behaviors		
Begins to understand complicated patterns of behavior		
Demonstrates the ability to communicate needs		
May say "no" to something they want		
May lose emotional control and have temper tantrums		
Shows self-conscious emotions such as shame, guilt, and shyness		
Becomes frustrated easily		
Nineteen to Twenty-Four Months		
Expresses affection to others spontaneously		
Acts to comfort others in distress		
Shows the emotions of pride and embarrassment		
Uses emotion words spontaneously in conversations or play		
Begins to show sympathy to another child or adult		
Becomes easily hurt by criticism		
Experiences a temper tantrum when goals are blocked, on occasion		
Associates facial expressions with simple emotional labels		
Twenty-Five to Thirty-Six Months		
Experiences increase in number of fears		
Begins to understand the consequences of basic emotions		
Learns skills for coping with strong emotions		
Seeks to communicate more feelings with specific words		
Shows signs of empathy and caring		
Loses control of emotions and throws temper tantrums		
Able to recover from temper tantrums		
Enjoys helping with chores such as cleaning up toys or carrying grocery bags		
Begins to show signs of readiness for toileting		
Desires that routines be carried out exactly as has been done in the past		

Additional Observations for Emotional Development

The developmental milestones listed are based on universal patterns of when various traits emerge. Because each child is unique certain traits may develop at an earlier or later age.

Anecdotal Record

SAMPLE ANECDOTAL RECORD

Child's name: __Reyshawn__ Date of birth: __5/13__

Observer's name: __Chris__ Observation date: __3/31__

Behavioral description of observation:

During diapering, Reyshawn took the clean diaper and covered his face. He then removed the diaper and began smiling and laughing.

Interpretation of observation:

Reyshawn was initiating a favorite game that we have played during diapering in the past. He is beginning to demonstrate advancements in his language and communication as well as his social skills.

SAMPLE ANECDOTAL RECORD

Child's name: _____ Date of birth:_____

Observer's name: _____ Observation date:_____

Behavioral description of observation:

Interpretation of observation:

Panel Documentation

A panel is a two-dimensional display to communicate with others the learning that occurred during an activity. Panels present the learning of a group of children; thus, different children and their work must be featured. For ease of reading, you should neatly handwrite or type your message. Then, adhere all sections mentioned in the following list on a foam board, poster board, or trifold board.

A panel should contain the following information:

♡ Title of the activity
♡ A record of the children's *actual* words while engaging with the materials or interacting with peers
♡ Artifacts to document representations of the children's thinking—drawings paintings, writings, and/or graphs—or photographs of the children's work on sculptures, creative drama/movements, or roles during dramatic play
♡ A narrative that highlights and explains what learning and interactions occurred

To fulfill the goal of communicating with others, the panel will need to be displayed in a prominent location. Invite others to look at and converse about the children's work. Include the children as part of the audience by reviewing their work as a way to promote language, cognitive, and social development. Also, build on the experience during future activities.

For additional resources on making panels, see:

Gandini, L., & Pope Edwards, C. (Eds.). (2001). *Bambini: The Italian approach to infant/toddler care.* New York: Teachers College Press.

Helm, J. H., Beneke, S., & Steinheimer, K. (1998). *Windows on learning: Documenting young children's work.* New York: Teachers College Press.

Pope Edwards, C., Gandini, L., & Forman, G. (Eds.). (1993). *The hundred languages of children.* Norwood, NJ: Ablex.

Lesson Plan

Name: _____ Date: _____

Developmental area: _____

Child's developmental goals:

Materials:

Preparation:

Nurturing strategies:

Variations:

Infant Daily Communication: Home to Center

Infant's name: _____ Parent's name: _____

Day/date: _____ Time of arrival: _____ Time of departure: _____

FILLED IN BY PARENT:

Infant seems: [ ] Normal, typical

[ ] Bit fussy

[ ] Not acting like usual

Infant slept: [ ] Soundly

[ ] Woke up several times

[ ] Did not sleep well

Infant ate: [ ] Meal before coming _____

[ ] Bottle or nursed before coming

[ ] Snack before coming

[ ] Nothing

Infant changed: [ ] Bowel movement Time _____

[ ] Wet Time _____

SPECIAL INSTRUCTIONS FOR TODAY:

_____

_____

_____

_____

Parent's signature: _____

Caregiver's signature: _____

Adapted with permission from New Horizon Child Care, Inc.

Infant Daily Communication: Center to Home

Date: _____ Check-in time: _____

Read infant's daily communication: Home to center _____

FILLED IN BY CAREGIVER:

Infant slept: Asleep _____   Awake _____

Asleep _____   Awake _____

Infant ate: Time _____   What _____   Amount _____

Time _____   What _____   Amount _____

Time _____   What _____   Amount _____

Infant changed: Time _____   Wet _____   Bowel movement _____

Time _____   Wet _____   Bowel movement _____

Time _____   Wet _____   Bowel movement _____

INTERACTIONS/ACTIVITIES: *(Description of adult interaction, developmental tasks, and activities that sustained child's interest)*

_____

_____

_____

NOTES TO PARENTS:

_____

_____

_____

Caregiver's signature: _____

Parent's signature: _____

We need: [ ] Diapers   [ ] Wipes   [ ] Formula   [ ] Baby food

[ ] Change of clothing   [ ] Blankets   [ ] Other: _____

Adapted with permission from New Horizon Child Care, Inc.